AFFILIATE MARKETING FOR BEGINNERS

UNLOCK ONLINE INCOME, AVOID COSTLY MISTAKES & PITFALLS, CREATE A SOLID FOUNDATION FOR LONG-TERM SUCCESS, AND ACHIEVE FINANCIAL INDEPENDENCE

AUDREY K ANDADO

IS THIS BOOK RIGHT FOR YOU?

Are you tired of living paycheck to paycheck, dreaming about financial freedom but feeling trapped by your reality?

Would you like to generate a stable online income but feel overwhelmed by which steps to take?

Do you find the prospect of navigating the digital world daunting, wondering if you're tech-savvy enough to succeed?

If you've answered 'yes' to any of these questions, you're not alone.

Research shows that 78% of workers in the US live paycheck to paycheck, which could lead to stress and a feeling of impending financial doom. The good news is, the internet is a vast and lucrative field ripe for harvesting - if you know the right strategies, that is.

Luckily for you, the blueprint to your financial success is right here in your hands.

Introducing 'Affiliate Marketing for Beginners: Unlock Online Income, Avoid Costly Mistakes & Pitfalls, Create a Solid

Foundation for Long-Term Success, and Achieve Financial Independence', a comprehensive guide that provides actionable insights on how to monetize your passion and earn a passively from the comfort of your home.

Here's just a taste of what you'll uncover in this guide:

The fundamentals of affiliate marketing, meticulously clarified for beginners so you can start your journey with confidence

A complete overview of the process to kick-starting your affiliate marketing venture - even with no initial capital

The key to identifying the right niche for YOU, based on your interests and goals, to boost your earning potential

How to master the art of engaging content creation, boosting your chances of transforming readers to clicks, and clicks to cash

An in-depth exploration of how to tackle the technical side of things, from setting up an affiliate marketing website that converts to using analytics to measure your success

Tips and tricks for SEO optimization to gain visibility and organic traffic

Strategies on how to stay motivated and patient, allowing your affiliate marketing venture to take root and flourish

The key mistakes to avoid as a beginner in affiliate marketing to ensure your journey towards online income is smooth and rewarding

An insightful primer on how ethical practice can amplify your success in the long run

And so much more!

Overcoming the feeling of being overwhelmed by the vastness of affiliate marketing or struggling to identify the right niche might seem daunting. But even with these hurdles, this guide provides the support, clarity, and step-by-step instruction to help you navigate your journey.

You're closer than you think to a life of financial freedom and independence. All it requires is the boldness to take the first step, the resilience to stay the course, and the right guide to light your path.

Through a mix of motivational content, practical advice, and conversational writing style, this book offers a doable blueprint for leveraging affiliate marketing with integrity and purpose - thereby earning you a sustainable online income.

If you're ready to unlock a life of financial freedom, seize control of your income, and redefine your future, start reading right now.

CONTENTS

INTRODUCTION

Three years ago, Alex was drowning in debt; his dreams of financial stability seemed farther out of his reach with each passing day. Desperately searching for a lifeline, he stumbled upon the affiliate marketing world. With determination and proper guidance, Alex cleared his debt and built a thriving online business that afforded him the freedom he never thought possible. This isn't just Alex's story—it could be yours.

I'm Audrey Andado, with a robust background in finance, entrepreneurship, and digital marketing strategies, I've navigated the highs and lows of online business ventures, transforming challenges into steppingstones for success. My passion lies in breaking down complex financial concepts into simple, actionable strategies anyone can follow, regardless of background or experience.

This book is the peak of my journey and the lessons I learned along the way. Its purpose is straightforward: to demystify the often-overwhelming world of affiliate marketing and provide a clear, step-by-step roadmap to unlock online income streams. I envision creating a community of confident, informed entrepreneurs ready to navigate the affiliate marketing landscape and build sustainable online businesses.

Let me set your expectations right from the start: I designed this book with you, the beginner, in mind. While the path to financial freedom through affiliate marketing requires dedication and persistence, I promise to make the journey as stress-free as possible. We will cover everything from selecting the right niche to creating engaging content, driving traffic to your site, and monetizing your affiliate marketing efforts with practical insights and real-world examples.

However, it's important to understand what this book will not cover. Advanced strategies that may overwhelm beginners, unnecessary technical jargon and niche-specific tactics with limited applicability will not find a home here. I focus on establishing a strong base for your venture into affiliate marketing, making sure it covers all essential aspects and is easily understandable.

From the outset, I want to emphasize the importance of ethical marketing. Building a business on honesty and transparency is not simply good practice—it's essential for long-term success. We'll explore how to promote products in a way that builds trust with your audience, fostering relationships that go beyond mere transactions.

I invite you to join me on this journey. This book isn't just a collection of information; it's your first step toward transforming your financial future. Approach it with an open mind, a willingness to learn and a readiness to apply new strategies. Together, let's unlock your potential, transform your life, and take control of your financial destiny through the power of affiliate marketing.

Remember, your path to financial independence starts with a single step. Let this book be that step. Engage fully, apply its lessons, and start paving your path to earning through affiliate marketing today. Are you ready to take control of your financial future?

CHAPTER 1

Affiliate marketing is a vibrant thread in a story of creativity, opportunity, and success in the fabric of digital business entrepreneurship. Affiliate marketing began during the rapid growth of the Internet. It was a bustling marketplace of ideas, rich with chances for discovery and utilization by those who could see its potential. Chapter 1 traces the growth of affiliate marketing from its early stages to its current glory. This chapter explains how the Internet has changed, what triggered its development, and how it helped people and businesses succeed. You'll learn how technology and creativity combine to make affiliate marketing an important part of online business.

1.1 THE EVOLUTION OF AFFILIATE MARKETING: FROM SIDE HUSTLE TO MAINSTREAM INCOME

Historical Overview

People often credit the origins of affiliate marketing to the mid-1990s when the Internet was initially commercialized. During this time, companies realized they could grow larger by rewarding people or groups that brought more website visitors. Companies started their first affiliate programs. This idea used the big, connected Internet world to create a helpful partnership between marketers and sellers.

Affiliate marketing has changed significantly since its beginnings, transitioning from simple income generation to a core pillar of many online business models. This change was not merely a function of time passing but was also a result of marketers learning how to adapt strategies based on how the online world was changing.

Growth Factors

Key developments have contributed to affiliate marketing's rise as a major player in the digital economy. The advent of search engines and the refinement of search engine optimization (SEO) gave affiliates a powerful tool to increase the visibility of their marketing efforts. This era of digital exploration made it possible for affiliates to attract targeted traffic with unprecedented precision and scale.

At the same time, social media platforms changed how people connect with online content, giving affiliates new ways to interact with audiences. Social media expanded the reach of affiliate marketers. They introduced the concept of influencer marketing, where people with large online followings could use their popularity to promote products or services, making affiliate marketing campaigns even more widespread and influential.

Additionally, technological advancements made many aspects of affiliate marketing automated and easy to navigate. This includes tracking how many people visit and make purchases through affiliate links and streamlining the management of online payments. These improvements opened affiliate marketing opportunities to a broader audience.

Success Stories

Numerous success stories increased affiliate marketing's popularity, proving its success and inspiring others to unlock its potential. Consider the case of a blogger who started with a passion for eco-friendly, sustainable living. She used affiliate marketing to turn her blog into a profitable platform promoting green products and services. Her success shows how content creators and sellers can work together in the affiliate marketing ecosystem, highlighting how authenticity and targeted content can yield substantial rewards.

Similarly, small businesses that used to rely only on traditional advertising have seen exponential growth by incorporating affiliate marketing into their sales strategies. By partnering with affiliates who deeply understand their niche markets, these businesses have connected with previously inaccessible audiences and converted them into customers.

Future Prospects

Several emerging trends are shaping affiliate marketing's future trajectory. The introduction of artificial intelligence and machine learning technologies allows marketers to personalize affiliate marketing efforts further. Tailored content and promotions based on individual consumer's unique preferences and behaviors increase website traffic by relating to customer needs.

Moreover, the ongoing expansion of e-commerce, accelerated by global events such as the COVID-19 pandemic, reinforced the importance and relevance of affiliate marketing in a digital-first world. The shift towards online shopping opened new avenues for affiliates to connect consumers with products and services, making affiliate marketing a key link in the online shopping world.

The spread of technology to a larger audience suggests it's getting easier for anyone to join affiliate marketing. This openness allows a broader range of people to participate and gain from the collaborative marketing world. This diversity makes affiliate marketing more exciting and encourages innovative ideas and competition, pushing it to keep improving and moving forward.

1.2 DECODING AFFILIATE MARKETING: TERMS AND CONCEPTS YOU NEED TO KNOW

Affiliate marketing includes a set of unique terms and ideas that are crucial for clear communication and effective planning. One important concept is "affiliate networks," which are online platforms that link merchants with affiliates. These networks create a mutually beneficial relationship where products meet promoters, and promoters discover profitable opportunities. They simplify the affiliate marketing process and provide analytics and tools that help affiliates improve their work and measure their achievements.

Delving further into the financial aspects, "commission rates" have become a key measure, indicating the portion of a sale price that affiliates earn as payment for their promotional work. These rates differ widely and are affected by factors like product type, the affiliate's performance, and the merchant's marketing plan. Also significant are "conversion rates," which gauge effectiveness by showing the percentage of visitors who take a desired action, like buying something, signing up for a newsletter, or completing a survey. Understanding and mastering these metrics enables affiliates to evaluate their performance and adjust their strategies for the best results.

Affiliates earn income in various ways, adapting to the dynamic digital environment. In the "pay-per-click" setup, affiliates get paid for each visitor they send to a merchant's site, regardless of whether a purchase occurs. This model thrives on high-volume traffic and demands affiliates to create compelling calls-to-action that resonate with their audience. On the other hand, the "pay-per-lead" method rewards affiliates for generating new leads through form submissions, free trials, or software downloads. Quality traffic and the match between the affiliate's content and the merchant's target audience are crucial in this model. At the top tier of affiliate compensation is the "pay-per-sale" system, where affiliates earn a commission for every sale made through their marketing efforts. This model showcases the mutual benefit of affiliate marketing, aligning affiliates' and merchants' interests toward boosting sales.

Yet, the financial complexities of affiliate marketing extend beyond these models. Affiliates must also navigate the technical aspects of the trade, including sophisticated "tracking methods" and "analytics." Modern affiliate marketing relies heavily on cookies and tracking codes to attribute sales to the correct affiliate. This process demands precision and transparency to maintain trust between all parties involved. Meanwhile, analytics platforms offer a wealth of data, revealing insights into user behavior, campaign performance, and market trends. Affiliates use this information to refine their strategies, target their efforts more effectively, and ultimately enhance their earning potential.

In this complex system, "industry standards" are the rules ensuring fairness, transparency, and ethical behavior. These standards include openly disclosing affiliate connections and banning deceptive advertising practices. Following these rules builds trust with consumers and safeguards the integrity of the affiliate marketing world. As digital platforms and consumer demands change, these standards are regularly updated to keep affiliate marketing a respected and effective option for digital entrepreneurship.

In the vast world of affiliate marketing, understanding these terms and concepts completely isn't just helpful; it's necessary. They're the words affiliates use to talk, plan, and succeed. By carefully learning and using these ideas, people can tap into the complete power of affiliate marketing, turning it from a mere income source into an essential component of their online achievements.

1.3 WHY AFFILIATE MARKETING: ANALYZING THE BENEFITS FOR BEGINNERS

In the digital business landscape, affiliate marketing guides those stepping into online ventures by being accessible and offering room for growth. Its appeal doesn't just lie in its ability to make money but also in how easy it is to get started, especially compared to other businesses that need a lot of money upfront. For newcomers, starting an affiliate marketing project primarily needs an online presence and a strong drive to succeed, making it a good choice for those with big dreams but limited resources.

What makes affiliate marketing so attractive is its low start-up costs. In contrast to traditional businesses that require a significant investment in things like stock, physical stores, or staff, affiliate marketing runs on a simple setup. Newcomers can build their online presence without spending a lot of money by making a blog or social media account and starting to promote products without buying or storing them. This equal opportunity lets people from different backgrounds dive into entrepreneurship without money holding them back.

Flexibility is a vital part of what makes affiliate marketing so attractive. It allows practitioners to explore different niches, products, and affiliate programs until they find the right fit. This flexibility lets affiliates align their marketing efforts with their interests or expertise, making their content more genuine and engaging for their audience. Whether into tech gadgets, eco-friendly living, or fashion, affiliates can customize their approach to connect with specific communities, blending their passions with making money.

Additionally, affiliates have choices not just in what they promote but also in how they do it. They can pick from various platforms like blogs, YouTube channels, or Instagram accounts to share their message, ensuring they reach their target audience effectively.

Beyond the initial appeal of starting with low costs and the freedom to chart their path, affiliate marketing has the power to generate passive income. Once affiliates have built an audience and earned trust, they can earn money without involvement. By creating strategic content attracting viewers, like evergreen blog posts, tutorials, and reviews, affiliates set up a cycle where promotion and income generation happen automatically. This ability to earn money while focusing on other parts of life brings a sense of financial freedom, turning time away from work into a chance to make money.

The scalability of affiliate marketing adds to its appeal by providing a way for significant growth without a corresponding increase in workload. As affiliates refine their strategies and better understand their audience, they can expand their reach by using more platforms, trying new niches, or working with different affiliate partners. This ability to multiply, built into how affiliate marketing works online, lets one person have a bigger impact than they could with traditional marketing methods. With each new piece of content, affiliates reach more potential customers and make more money. This scalability, combined with the rewards based on performance, creates a powerful environment for driven individuals to achieve and even exceed their financial goals.

In this space where ambition meets opportunity, affiliate marketing shows how the digital era can transform lives. It offers financial freedom for those willing to learn the ins and outs of online marketing. With its easy entry, flexible approach, potential for passive income, and ability to scale up, affiliate marketing isn't just a business idea but a journey toward personal and financial development. Affiliate marketing is a promising starting point for newcomers wanting to navigate the complexities of the online economy, encouraging them to discover their entrepreneurial spirit to its fullest.

1.4 SETTING REALISTIC EXPECTATIONS: WHAT AFFILIATE MARKETING CAN AND CANNOT DO FOR YOU

In affiliate marketing, newcomers often envision quick success and easy money, but this perception can be misleading. It's important to gently lift this veil of anticipation to see the reality beneath

—one filled with potential but grounded in the need for hard work and patience. Understanding what affiliate marketing can offer is essential for making meaningful progress and avoiding disappointment.

The timeline for becoming profitable in affiliate marketing varies widely among individuals. While stories of rapid success are enticing, they are more the exception than the rule. A more realistic view sees affiliate marketing compared to tending a garden—it takes time, care, and attention to detail. Just like planting seeds, your affiliate marketing efforts need time to grow. At first, progress may seem slow as you establish your presence and connect with your audience. This period is crucial and can last from several months to a year. During this time, focus on building your online presence, refining your marketing strategies, and building relationships with your audience. Profitability comes as a result of consistent effort rather than sudden luck.

In conversations about earning potential, there's a popular belief in affiliate marketing's ability to generate easy wealth. These myths, though tempting, often distort the reality of what's achievable. Income from affiliate marketing varies widely and is affected by factors like which niche you choose, how effective your marketing strategies are, and the size and engagement level of your audience. For some, affiliate marketing brings in extra money as a supplement to their main earnings. For others, with dedication and smart strategies, it can become their main source of income. However, reaching this level of success demands a deep understanding of your audience, the skill to create valuable content, and the ability to navigate the constantly changing digital marketing scene. While the potential to earn big exists, it requires ongoing and focused effort.

The hard work and dedication required to build and run a successful affiliate marketing business often get overlooked amid online success stories. Yet, this work is the foundation of any prosperous affiliate marketing venture. From choosing a niche and building a platform to creating content, promoting products, and interacting with your audience, affiliate marketing demands significant time and effort. This effort goes beyond what's immediately visible—it includes learning new marketing methods, analyzing performance data, and staying updated with trends in your niche. Success in affiliate marketing doesn't come from luck but from persistent, consistent work.

Consideration of affiliate marketing's limitations is crucial. The digital world offers many opportunities but not without fierce competition. Standing out in a crowded market requires creativity and a willingness to try new approaches. Additionally, your success in affiliate marketing can be affected by changes in merchant policies, like commission rates or program terms, which may impact your earnings and require you to adjust your strategy. These constraints can be discouraging. However, understanding these constraints increases your ability to be prepared to navigate these challenges flexibly and resiliently.

Knowing affiliate marketing's potential and limitations gives you a clear direction for your where to invest your efforts. Success in this field requires persistence, adaptability, and a strong drive for growth. Being realistic about what you can achieve helps you tackle challenges and seize opportunities effectively.

1.5 NAVIGATING THE LEGAL LANDSCAPE OF AFFILIATE MARKETING

Understanding the legal side of affiliate marketing is vital in the complex online world where ambition meets digital skills. Transparency, respecting privacy, and protecting intellectual property aren't just ethical ideas—they're essential rules that keep your affiliate work in good standing. Legal rules in these areas function as both a guide and a safety net, ensuring that you follow the law and uphold high standards of ethics and integrity throughout your affiliate marketing journey.

Disclaimer

The information provided to you about legal and ethical considerations is merely food for thought. In the ever-evolving legal and regulatory landscape new laws and considerations appear over time. Considerations are presented at a high level to make it easier for affiliate marketing beginners to understand. The information presented to you throughout this book is advice and should not be construed as formal legal counsel. With that, the author is not liable for anything that results from any actions taken (or not taken) by the reader after going through this book. When in doubt, always consult certified legal counsel in your area.

Disclosure Requirements

Central to the legal aspect of affiliate marketing is the requirement for clear disclosure of affiliate relationships. Based on transparency and consumer protection, this rule requires that affiliates inform their audience whenever their content is sponsored or contains affiliate links. The purpose of this rule is to maintain trust between the affiliate and the audience by avoiding any confusion about the nature of the content. Disclosures should be noticeable and close to affiliate links, ensuring they are not lost among other text or hidden in obscure webpage parts. This disclosure is a declaration of integrity, signaling to your audience that transparency guides your actions.

Privacy Laws

The digital era's advanced data-gathering capabilities led to the implementation of strict privacy laws aimed at protecting personal information. For affiliates, these laws require careful handling of data, especially when collecting email addresses, tracking user actions, or using cookies for analytics and customization. Examples of such laws include the General Data Protection Regulation (GDPR) in the EU and the California Consumer Privacy Act (CCPA) in the US, which dictate how personal data should be collected, processed, and stored. To comply with these laws, affiliates need a transparent privacy policy that explains the purpose and nature of data collection and obtains explicit consent when necessary. Following these regulations ensures legal compliance and builds trust with your audience, showing them that their privacy is a top priority.

Intellectual Property

In the vast expanse of the Internet, where content holds significant sway, respecting intellectual property rights is crucial. Affiliates, as creators and promoters of content, must navigate copyright and trademark laws carefully. This means ensuring they don't infringe on others' rights when using images, videos, text, or trademarks. While using popular music, branded visuals, or copyrighted material to enhance affiliate content might be tempting, it can lead to legal consequences and damage your reputation. It's important to responsibly source materials by choosing royalty-free assets or obtaining proper permissions for copyrighted content before it is used. Likewise, when using trademarks in affiliate content, it's crucial to avoid implying any endorsement or affiliation the trademark owner hasn't explicitly granted. If you are unsure about whether the content is usable or not, ask the owner or research limitations to its use. Taking this careful approach to intellectual property minimizes legal risks and shows your dedication to ethical content creation.

International Considerations

The global nature of the digital market adds layers of complexity to the legal aspects of affiliate marketing. The Internet has no boundaries, meaning content can reach audiences across legal jurisdictions. This worldwide reach requires understanding how legal requirements for affiliate marketing may vary in different regions. For example, disclosure standards or privacy regulations differ from one country to another, imposing unique obligations on data handling and consent.

To navigate this international legal landscape, affiliate marketers must proactively stay informed about the legal standards that apply to targeted audiences. This might involve tailoring disclosures to meet specific requirements in different places or adjusting data collection practices to comply with various privacy laws. This global perspective on legal compliance helps minimize the risk of unintentionally breaking local laws and shows respect for the diverse audience that the digital world brings.

In the intricacies of the affiliate marketing environment, where ambitions and ethical considerations come together, the legal framework sets the stage. It's a realm where transparency, privacy respect, intellectual property rights adherence, and understanding of international legal nuances guide every action. Navigating this terrain with care and integrity ensures that your affiliate marketing efforts are successful and conducted in a way that honors the trust of your audience and the legal rules set up to protect it.

1.6 ETHICAL MARKETING: BUILDING TRUST WITH YOUR AUDIENCE

Trust becomes incredibly important in an affiliate marketing environment, where transactions happen online and relationships are built without in-person contact. The digital marketplace is vast and full of options, which can overwhelm consumers as they navigate various choices. In this complicated environment, ethical marketing practices aren't just the right thing to do morally— they're also crucial for standing out and building a community of loyal followers engaged with your content.

Transparency

Transparency forms the foundation of trust in affiliate marketing. Following legal disclosure rules demonstrates respect for your audience and confirms your integrity. When affiliates are open about partnerships and the content they share, it sends a message that values the intelligence and independence of consumers. This honesty turns promotion into an act of integrity, encouraging your audience to make informed choices with clear, straightforward information. The effect of this transparency is profound, creating a basis for a relationship built on trust and mutual respect.

Authenticity

Transparency and authenticity are closely linked qualities that give life to your affiliate marketing efforts and infuse them with meaning and sincerity. Authenticity stands out as a symbol of relatability and honesty in a digital world often criticized for being superficial. Committing to promoting only products or services that align with your beliefs and experiences demonstrates your integrity. This authenticity resonates with your audience, who seek guidance from a trustworthy source whose opinions and endorsements are sincere and not driven by profit. This authenticity results in a stronger connection with your audience, going beyond just transactions and building a sense of community and shared values.

Value Addition

In addition to the mechanics of promotion and compensation details, providing real value to your audience is crucial. This principle challenges affiliates to look beyond making a profit to seeing content as a way to enrich and empower their audience's lives. The content should aim to educate, inspire, or solve problems through informative articles, thoughtful reviews, or helpful tutorials, giving the audience something meaningful beyond simple product promotions. Your role is transformed from just being an affiliate marketer to becoming a trusted advisor and leader in your field. This dedication builds a loyal following dependent on you for recommendations, guidance, and inspiration.

Long-term Relationships

The combination of transparency, authenticity, and providing value leads to building lasting relationships with your audience—

relationships based on trust, loyalty, and mutual respect. These relationships show the effectiveness of ethical marketing practices, going beyond individual transactions to create ongoing engagement and support. By consistently following these principles, you create an environment where your audience feels valued and heard, their needs are prioritized, and their loyalty is earned through genuine efforts. This ethical marketing approach ensures that your success isn't short-lived but sustainably rooted in lasting connections.

In the complex world of affiliate marketing, ethical practices act as a compass, guiding you toward success measured not only in sales and commissions but also in audience trust and loyalty. This journey involves transparency, authenticity, adding value, and building lasting relationships. It brings rewards beyond financial gains, satisfying you to know that your success is built on integrity and the positive impact you make on others' lives.

1.7 CHOOSING YOUR PATH: DIFFERENT AFFILIATE MARKETING MODELS EXPLORED

The direction you choose in affiliate marketing will shape your online business. With its many complexities, this decision demands careful consideration of the different models available, each offering unique benefits and challenges.

Niche-focused

A niche is a specialized area focused on a specific kind of product or service targeted at a narrower audience. Choosing to specialize in a specific niche stakes a claim in a carefully selected part of the digital world, establishing expertise and interest in that area. This approach allows for a deeper exploration of a subject, offering the chance to become a respected authority within that field. Whether it's outdoor gear, vegan beauty products, or financial tools, focusing on a niche enables the creation of content that deeply connects with a targeted audience, increasing the chances of conversion due to shared interests.

However, committing to a niche also brings challenges, such as market saturation and limitations on audience size. The online space is full of voices vying for attention, and finding a unique angle within a popular niche can be like finding a rare grain of sand on a vast beach. Additionally, narrowing the focus to a niche may limit audience growth, keeping efforts confined within the boundaries of that chosen niche.

Product-centric vs. Audience-centric

Choosing between focusing on products or audiences presents a critical decision point for affiliate marketers. A product-centric approach emphasizes promoting specific products, often driven by attractive commission rates or personal enthusiasm. This strategy involves creating detailed, convincing content that showcases the product's benefits and features, potentially leading to higher conversion rates among those already interested in buying.

In contrast, an audience-centric approach centers on a specific audience segment's needs, interests, and challenges, aiming to build trust and connection beyond individual products. This strategy involves selecting products and services that cater to a range of audience needs and fostering loyalty and a community for sustained engagement. While this approach requires extensive research and a deep understanding of the audience, it offers the flexibility to adapt to changing market trends and audience preferences without relying solely on the success of a single product.

Content-driven

Content holds significant importance in today's digital age. Embracing a content-focused approach to affiliate marketing offers a reliable path to success. This approach revolves around creating valuable and captivating content that attracts and retains an audience. It provides fertile ground for affiliate promotions to integrate into the informative or entertaining content provided naturally. Whether it's detailed product reviews, instructional guides, or engaging stories seamlessly incorporating product mentions, content-focused affiliate marketing prioritizes giving substance to the audience over direct sales pitches.

The sustainability of this approach lies in its ability to cultivate a dedicated following that returns for the content itself, with affiliate promotions enhancing rather than overpowering the overall experience. However, the effectiveness of this strategy depends on consistently delivering top-notch content that stands out amidst a sea of content, which demands significant investments of time, creativity, and sometimes financial resources.

Influencer-driven

With the rise of social media's influence on consumer culture, the influencer-driven affiliate marketing model has become increasingly powerful. This model relies on influencers' established trust and connection with their followers, leveraging their ability to impact purchasing decisions through genuine endorsements and personalized stories. Whether through posts on Instagram, videos on YouTube, or challenges on TikTok, influencers can bring affiliate products to life by showcasing them in the context of their daily lives or genuine interests, making them more appealing and persuasive.

This model thrives on the mutual relationship between influencers and their audience, with influencers as a link that connects affiliate products with potential buyers in a way that traditional ads cannot achieve. However, the challenge lies in identifying influencers whose audience demographics, values, and interests align well with the promoted affiliate products. Moreover, the influencer-driven model requires careful negotiation and a clear understanding of expectations from both parties to ensure that the partnership is mutually beneficial and maintains the authenticity that defines successful influencer marketing.

When navigating the affiliate marketing world, the model you choose—or a blend of different models—determines the strategies used and the connections built with your audience. Whether diving deep into a niche, prioritizing products or audience interests, creating captivating content, or collaborating with influencers, your path mirrors your marketing principles and goals. Each model has its benefits and hurdles, demanding a customized strategy that matches your strengths, values, and aspirations for progress in the constantly changing affiliate marketing landscape.

THE SYMPHONY OF AFFILIATE MARKETING: UNDERSTANDING ITS PLAYERS AND THEIR ROLES

Affiliate marketing is a steadfast beacon of opportunity and collaboration in a world where digital landscapes constantly shift. Picture a symphony orchestra, each musician playing a distinct yet crucial role, their contributions blending into a harmonious whole. This analogy mirrors the affiliate marketing ecosystem, where diverse entities—affiliates, merchants, networks, and consumers—unite, each playing their part in creating a seamless, profitable performance. Understanding these roles and the dynamics between them is similar to conducting this orchestra, guiding each element to achieve a collective success that resonates with audiences everywhere.

2.1 THE AFFILIATE MARKETING ECOSYSTEM: PLAYERS AND ROLES

Affiliates: At the forefront of affiliate marketing are the affiliates, comparable to conductors in an orchestra. They carefully curate and create content seamlessly, incorporating products into compelling stories that are captivating and inspiring to their audience. Through blogs, social media platforms, or videos, they introduce their followers to products or services, expertly guiding them through the purchasing journey with their knowledge and understanding. Their income is directly tied to commissions earned from successful promotions. For instance, take a food blogger who skillfully integrates kitchen gadgets into their content through detailed recipes and captivating narratives, effectively boosting sales and earning commissions. This role demands creativity, strategic planning, and a deep understanding of the product and the target audience.

Merchants: On the other side are the merchants who compose the score for this symphony. They are the creators of products or services seeking a broader audience. They view affiliates as partners in expanding their reach, spotlighting their offerings for a receptive audience. For merchants, affiliates offer a cost-effective marketing channel, with commissions tied directly to sales, ensuring a measurable return on investment that traditional advertising often struggles to achieve. For example, a small artisan coffee roastery might collaborate with affiliates to access a wider market, leveraging the authenticity and reach of coffee enthusiasts and reviewers.

Networks: The affiliate networks act as the orchestrators that ensure harmony among affiliates and merchants. These platforms serve as a meeting point, a marketplace where merchants list their programs and affiliates discover opportunities aligned with their interests and audience. In addition to matchmaking, networks provide essential tools for tracking, payment processing, and performance analysis, simplifying the operational aspects of affiliate marketing. They guarantee that each affiliate's contributions are accurately measured and rewarded, like ensuring each musician's role in an orchestra is acknowledged and valued.

Consumers: The audience at the heart of the symphony's success is the key to determining the ecosystem's effectiveness. Their actions—clicking links, making purchases, subscribing to services—generate the revenue that sustains the entire system. Their preferences and actions significantly influence the strategies and content employed by affiliates, guiding product selections and creating promotional materials. In an era where consumers face many options, their engagement and loyalty stand as prized achievements earned through delivering relevant, valuable, and trustworthy experiences.

Visual Element: An intricate infographic visually outlines the functions of affiliates, merchants, networks, and consumers within the affiliate marketing ecosystem. Each element is interconnected, illustrating the flow of information, products, and commissions and encapsulating the interdependent relationships that power the system.

The affiliate marketing ecosystem flourishes through cooperation, where every participant contributes to a shared narrative of success based on their roles and interactions. Affiliates bring their content and audience understanding; merchants offer innovative products, networks facilitate collaborations, and consumers fuel demand, crafting a narrative reverberating throughout the digital realm. Grasping this ecosystem isn't just about identifying roles but understanding the intricate dynamics and the subtle interplays that merge separate contributions into a unified, harmonious entity.

2.2 UNDERSTANDING YOUR AUDIENCE: THE KEY TO AFFILIATE SUCCESS

In the complex fabric of affiliate marketing, the brightest threads aren't woven from overarching marketing plans or subtle network connections but from a deep grasp of one's audience. Unraveling an elaborate puzzle requires careful attention, and a thorough understanding of the audience's wants, requirements, and obstacles influences every choice and step.

Audience Analysis

The first step in gaining a deep understanding of the audience involves a thorough audience analysis. This isn't just about collecting basic information; it's about diving deep into the minds of potential customers. It requires keen observation of how they behave online, listening closely to discussions in forums and comments, and paying attention to what they share on social media. Tools and platforms that track user engagement, along with analytics software, act as guides in this journey, providing data that gives a full view of who the audience is when it is combined with qualitative insights. This analysis reveals what the audience does and why they do it, uncovering their motivations, concerns, and goals.

Creating Personas

The next crucial step requires creating detailed audience personas from the wealth of audience analysis information. Though fictional, these personas are based on the gathered data and represent ideal customers within a larger audience segment. Building these personas involves crafting stories that breathe life into these examples, outlining their demographics, daily routines, challenges, and how the advertised products play a role in their lives. This process goes beyond merely categorizing audience groups; it adds a human touch to the data, transforming numbers and trends into relatable characters with which both the affiliate and their audience can emotionally connect. Developing these personas guides content strategies and promotional approaches, ensuring every message resonates with the intended audience segment.

Engagement Strategies

With personas created, the focus transitions to establishing genuine connections through engagement strategies to build trust and cultivate loyalty. This phase involves an interactive process between creating tailored content that addresses the personas' needs and interests and actively engaging with the audience by listening and responding to their feedback. Engagement goes beyond mere transactions; it fosters a sense of community based on shared interests that provide value extending beyond product suggestions. Strategies can take various forms, such as informative content that solves problems, entertaining posts that uplift, or inspiring stories that motivate. Social media serves as a platform for this engagement, enabling immediate interaction that strengthens the bond between the affiliate and their audience.

The foundation of your dynamic engagement strategy lies in authenticity and consistency. Authenticity ensures the affiliate's voice and values remain true, fostering trust and reliability among the audience. Conversely, consistency reinforces the audience's trust by demonstrating the affiliate's ongoing commitment, establishing a rhythm and expectation that encourages continued engagement. When combined, these elements create a positive cycle of engagement where each interaction strengthens the relationship, making the audience more open to affiliate recommendations.

Feedback Loops

Creating feedback loops is essential to maintain engagement and keep affiliate efforts relevant. These loops act as pathways for ongoing improvement, allowing affiliates to adjust their strategies based on direct input from their audience. Setting up feedback loops involves gathering opinions through surveys, monitoring comments on content, and analyzing user interaction data. Positive and negative feedback provides valuable insights for refining content, modifying promotional tactics, and reassessing product choices. This process shows the audience that their input is valued and they play a role in shaping the affiliate's narrative.

Furthermore, feedback loops highlight the adaptable nature of affiliate marketing, where strategies evolve to match changing audience preferences and market trends. They ensure that the affiliate's actions align with the audience's wants, creating an environment of continual relevance and sustained engagement. This adaptability, driven by insights from the audience, guarantees that affiliate marketing stays effective and impactful, meeting the audience's evolving needs and expectations.

Grasping the audience's essence is the central point shaping all affiliate marketing plans. It requires effort, attention, empathy, and a readiness to change. Knowing your audience is the key to affiliate prosperity, turning ordinary promotions into meaningful connections that boost sales and foster long-term bonds. This journey is both tough and fulfilling, providing insights beyond marketing and diving into how people connect with the digital realm and each other.

2.3 UNDERSTANDING YOUR TARGET AUDIENCE: DEMOGRAPHICS AND PSYCHOGRAPHICS

In affiliate marketing's complex fabric, success hinges on deeply grasping one's audience. This goes beyond surface-level interactions, diving into demographics and psychographics where data guides marketers. The journey begins with gathering demographic data including age, gender, location, education, et cetera, from tools like social media metrics, website stats, and surveys. Each interaction paints a picture, revealing preferences that shape tailored strategies. It's not just about collecting information; marketers must interpret this data wisely, letting it guide without limiting, and crafting strategies that connect emotionally with the diverse audience segments.

Along with gathering demographic data, there's the crucial task of psychographic profiling, a deep dive into the thoughts and feelings of the target audience. Unlike demographics, psychographics offers a multifaceted view of motivations, values, and lifestyles. This profiling requires empathy, prioritizing, listening, and understanding. Surveys delving into deeper preferences, social media interactions unveiling personal values, and engagement metrics hinting at lifestyle choices are tools for creating these profiles. Each profile, showcasing motivations and values, acts as a roadmap, guiding how content and products can align with audience desires. Building these profiles isn't an endpoint but a starting point, forming the basis for strategies that adapt and refine with the audience changes, ensuring the affiliate's offerings stay meaningful and relatable.

The next step is to segment the audience using insights from demographic and psychographic analysis. Segmentation is a strategic way to group the audience into subsets with unique preferences, challenges, and needs by organizing data in a meaningful way. Segmenting helps target content and promotions accurately, ensuring they reach those most likely to get involved and take action. It acknowledges the audience's diversity, respecting each segment's differences and adjusting strategies to fit their needs. Segmentation criteria vary widely, from behaviors and purchase history to engagement levels and content preferences. This segmentation is flexible, adapting to audience changes and market trends, showing a commitment to staying relevant and delivering tailored content and offerings.

This stage marks the transition from planning to action, where insights from demographic and psychographic analysis and audience segmentation are implemented. The focus is aligning marketing efforts with a deep understanding of the audience. Content strategies are refined to match the interests, tone, and style preferred by different audience segments, boosting engagement and building stronger connections. Similarly, promotional strategies are customized, and the most effective channels and methods are chosen to reach and sway targeted segments. These insights impact content and promotion. They influence product choices and how they're presented, ensuring they meet the audience's wants and challenges. It's a careful balancing act that maintains relevance and genuineness, ensuring the affiliate's voice remains authentic while addressing audience needs.

This journey through demographics, psychographics, segmentation, and application of insights is foundational to affiliate marketing success. It's a process characterized by empathy, accuracy, creativity, and analysis, where understanding the audience is the cornerstone of all strategic actions. This thorough exploration of the audience's world, where data transforms into understanding and understanding into strategy, guarantees that affiliate marketing efforts are meaningful and impactful, resonating deeply with the audience and building lasting connections beyond mere transactions.

2.4 ESSENTIAL TOOLS FOR EVERY AFFILIATE MARKETER

Essential tools serve as navigational aids across affiliate marketing's complex structure. These tools offer direction and understanding across the expansive digital realm. These tools, diverse in their uses and goals, empower marketers to maneuver and excel amidst the competitive nature of online business. Whether uncovering impactful keywords or creating captivating content, each tool plays a fundamental role in achieving success, propelling strategies onward and paving the way for audience interaction and conversion.

Keyword Research Tools

The goal for high visibility in the vast online world starts with carefully choosing keywords. Keywords act like guiding lights, attracting specific visitors to one's online space. Tools for researching keywords become invaluable partners in this effort, giving insights into how people search online and what they prefer. These digital helpers provide a wide view of keyword landscapes, showing which terms are popular and how competitive they are. They highlight opportunities where demand is high, but competition is low, allowing affiliates to position their content where it's most likely to be seen in search engine results. Armed with this information, affiliates create content that answers their audience's questions and matches their interests, making their digital presence stand out like prominent landmarks in the vastness of the Internet, capturing attention and keeping it engaged.

SEO Tools

With keyword research completed, attention turns to Search Engine Optimization. SEO is a refining process where content is adjusted and structured to catch the notice of search engines. With their complex algorithms and analysis capabilities, SEO tools provide vital insights into this optimization journey, assessing aspects like site speed and mobile friendliness. They examine the structure of a website, identifying elements that either boost or hinder visibility on search engines. Details like meta tags, images, and internal links on web pages are thoroughly assessed, with suggestions to enhance the content's relevance and ease of access. These tools light the way toward optimization and allow for ongoing monitoring and fine-tuning, ensuring that a website's visibility adapts to the constantly evolving search engine algorithms. Through this systematic process, affiliates ensure their digital platforms shine brightly in the competitive online market, attracting audiences with the promise of relevant and easily discoverable content.

Content Creation Tools

At the core of affiliate marketing is content, the tool through which products are introduced, and stories are narrated. Various content creation tools empower affiliates to turn ideas into digital realities, creating pieces that captivate, educate, and convince. These tools range from software for designing graphics that reinforce visual concepts to platforms for editing videos that spin stories into motion. Content calendars and management systems provide organization and structure, enabling strategic planning and distribution of content across multiple platforms. With these resources, affiliates craft individual content pieces and build entire ecosystems of engagement, where every post, video, and image works together to enthrall the audience and guide them from curiosity to action. The quality of content reflects the affiliate's dedication to their audience, boosting their reputation in the digital world and distinguishing them as creators of value and providers of solutions.

Analytics Tools

In affiliate marketing, data is like a reflection and a crystal ball, showing how well past efforts worked while giving hints about future possibilities. Sophisticated analytics tools break down and understand digital interactions, providing ongoing insights into a website's performance and content. These tools follow every visitor's journey, from their first click to their final action, providing a detailed view of their behavior and engagement level. They track how well digital platforms do, pinpointing what content connects with people and which strategies lead to conversions. Armed with this information, affiliates fine-tune their methods, improving what's effective and reassessing what's not. This ongoing process of analyzing and adjusting fuels growth in affiliate marketing, pushing strategies to match the audience's needs better. Through analytics, affiliates measure their success and refine their approach, ensuring their work makes an impact.

In this complex orchestra of affiliate marketing, the tools marketers use are precision instruments and tools for creativity, helping produce strategies that resonate and content that captures attention. Starting with the basics like keyword research and SEO optimization, moving to innovative tasks like content creation, and ending with analytical tasks including performance tracking, each tool plays a crucial part in achieving success. They allow affiliates to navigate the digital landscape confidently, ensuring every effort is well-informed, every strategy is targeted, and every piece of content moves toward engaging and converting the audience.

2.5 ANALYZING MARKET DEMAND: TOOLS AND TECHNIQUES

Understanding what customers want is like finding your way through a maze, where every twist gives new clues and challenges. To connect with what people are looking for, affiliate marketers use advanced tools and methods that uncover the details of customer demand. This isn't just about gathering data; it's a thoughtful strategy that guides everything the affiliate does, from choosing a specific market to creating content and promoting products.

Keyword Research

The first step is delving into keyword research, using digital tools as a guide. These tools are powered by algorithms that sort through data, revealing what terms and phrases consumers use when looking for things online. For example, an affiliate marketer may use tools to identify the top ten keywords consumers search on Amazon for a particular product. This information is invaluable, showing how often people search for things and what they want to achieve. By studying these keywords, affiliates see what consumers think and why. This insight shapes their content plans, helping them create material that meets consumers where they are, addressing their queries, and providing solutions that truly connect.

Trend Analysis

Alongside keyword research, trend analysis is a vital strategy that uses tools like Google Trends to monitor changes in consumer interest across time. Unlike static data, this analysis gives a dynamic view of how interests change—whether due to seasons, global happenings, or larger cultural shifts. This data is incredibly valuable for affiliate marketers, allowing them to predict market changes and adjust their promotions to match emerging trends. By keeping ahead of these shifts, affiliates don't just advertise products but also become trusted voices whose content and recommendations show a keen awareness of how the market evolves.

Audience Needs Assessment

Moving beyond numbers, there's a qualitative side to understanding what the audience wants. This involves digging below the surface details into the deeper aspects of consumer desires. Forums, social media platforms, and surveys are key places for this exploration, where people openly share what they're unhappy about, what they want, and what they're missing. By engaging in these online spaces, affiliates hear directly from the market, gathering insights beyond product selection to shape their marketing approach. This active listening creates a bond with the audience, turning the affiliate from an outsider into a trusted part of the community they serve. In this environment, the affiliate fine-tunes its offerings, making sure they meet current needs and can anticipate what customers will want in the future.

Demand Validation

The final piece of this intricate puzzle is demand validation, a critical step where ideas are tested in real-world scenarios. There are various methods for validation, like launching minimal viable products (MVPs) to see if there's interest or studying competitors' success to gauge demand indirectly. This phase aims to confirm ideas and assess their potential before fully committing, ensuring that the chosen niche, product, or content strategy has genuine potential to attract and convert customers. It checks against assumptions, ensuring the affiliate's efforts are based on real market needs. This validation is an ongoing process, a cycle of testing, refining, and improving that keeps the affiliate's offerings relevant and effective.

In the bigger picture, these tools and strategies serve as the foundation for successful affiliate marketing tactics. They provide insights into what the market wants and how it behaves, guiding decisions ranging from niche selection to content creation and product promotion. This process demands precision and adaptability, ensuring the affiliate's efforts are targeted and in tune with the market's current state and future trends. It's a blend of data analysis and creative intuition that shapes the affiliate's journey toward market success through the maze of consumer demand.

As we close this exploration of market demand analysis, it's clear that an affiliate marketer's journey is one of continuous learning and adaptation. The insights gained from keyword research, trend analysis, audience needs assessment, and demand validation illuminate the path forward, offering a roadmap for engaging with the market in a meaningful and impactful way. This foundation, built on understanding market demand, sets the stage for the strategies and tactics explored in the following chapters, guiding affiliates toward success in their digital endeavors.

CARVING YOUR NICHE IN THE DIGITAL MARKETPLACE

E ach decision made in your affiliate marketing journey refines the unique identity of your niche. Unlike physical materials, digital opportunities are boundless, offering endless potential. It's like a gardener planning a garden; today's decisions affect tomorrow's blossoms. Your niche choice is crucial in affiliate marketing—it defines your audience, content, and promoted products. This decision requires self-reflection and market study, blending your interests with what consumers seek.

3.1 THE ART OF NICHE SELECTION: FINDING YOUR PLACE IN THE MARKET

Niche Identification

At the heart of niche selection lies identifying areas of personal passion that intersect with market demand. Imagine a Venn diagram where one circle represents your interests and the other the needs or desires of a specific market segment. The overlap between these circles is where a viable niche can be found. For instance, if you're sincerely interested in sustainable living and notice a growing trend in eco-friendly travel, this intersection could represent a fertile niche. Tools such as Google Trends or social listening platforms can offer insights into these growing trends, allowing you to pinpoint areas where your interests align with emerging market demands.

Alignment with Personal Interest

It's crucial to connect your niche with what genuinely interests you. This connection ensures that your affiliate marketing path is fueled by passion and expertise, qualities that resonate with audiences and build their trust. For instance, compare someone promoting fitness gear due to a personal training background versus someone uninterested in fitness. The former brings authenticity to their recommendations and can share personal stories, enriching their content. This authenticity attracts audiences looking for trustworthy guidance, laying a strong groundwork for lasting success.

Competitive Analysis

Analyzing your competition gives you a broad perspective of what's happening in your niche, showing you where the opportunities are and what challenges you might face. This process involves figuring out the major niche players, studying how they create and share content, and seeing how they connect with their audiences. Tools like SEMrush or Ahrefs can give you data about your competitors' website traffic, the keywords they rank for, and the links to their sites, which can help you figure out how to stand out.

For instance, in the eco-friendly travel industry, many competitors focus on budget-friendly travel options. You can set yourself apart in the market by positioning your brand as a provider of luxurious, eco-friendly travel experiences. The niche is the same; however, you set yourself apart from your competitors by creating a unique marketing approach.

Niche Validation

The final step in picking your niche is validation, which means making sure it's both profitable and interesting to your audience. To do this, you can try out your niche idea with minimal viable content (MVC), like a few blog posts or social media posts, to see how people react. You can also directly ask your audience for feedback through surveys or polls on social media to better understand their level of interest and specific needs. For example, if you're thinking about focusing on eco-friendly travel, start by writing blog posts about different aspects of sustainable travel and see which topics get the most attention and interaction. This feedback loop helps you fine-tune your niche, making sure it's a strong foundation for building a successful affiliate marketing business.

Self-Evaluation of Niche Selection

Choosing a niche in the digital market requires both creativity and precision. You must balance what you love with what's practical for the market. This process involves carefully looking at your interests, understanding what's trending, keeping an eye on competitors, and methodically checking if your niche idea is viable. When all these aspects work together, your niche reflects your unique perspective and skills, attracting audiences looking for guidance.

Research popular niches and identify one or more where you have genuine passion and interest. Once your top niche candidates are identified, you can delve deeper into their characteristics. Examples of popular niches include Health and Wellness, Online Gaming, Technology, Pets, Travel and Leisure, Arts and Crafts, Education, Food and Beverage, Beauty and Fashion, and Personal Finance. Of course, the number of niches continues to expand as customer needs diversify.

Evaluate your personal potential for success in the niche. Assess the amount of time you can invest, skills and equipment needed, and startup costs. Evaluate how long it takes for affiliate marketers within the niche to earn profits after creating their business. Can you sustain the dedication and budget required for the total time between starting up and profitability? Conducting an honest self-evaluation of your capabilities and resources based on researched niche requirements is a critical part of any business startup.

3.2 THE POWER OF NICHE SELECTION IN AFFILIATE MARKETING

In today's digital era, where the internet is flooded with content, standing out is a necessity for survival and success. The niche an affiliate picks acts like their flag planted firmly in the digital soil, signaling their expertise and the community they want to help. This deliberate choice creates a chain of events that shapes the affiliate's path. It dictates the kind of audience they attract, the content they make, and, ultimately, how profitable their efforts will be. A well-chosen niche is a guiding light, bringing in a focused, engaged audience with shared interests or problems. This makes marketing efforts more effective and targeted. Conversely, a poorly chosen niche can lead to scattered efforts, an unfocused audience, and lower returns. So, choosing the right niche is crucial—it's the foundation for the affiliate's digital success.

Several factors must be considered, carefully ensuring the chosen niche has growth potential. Market demand is a key factor, indicating whether there's an audience actively looking for information, solutions, or products in that niche. This demand is crucial for generating traffic, engagement, and conversions. However, more than just demand is needed for a profitable niche. The level of competition in that niche also needs scrutiny. While high interest shows a healthy market, too much competition can make it tough for new players. Striking a balance where demand and competition allow for growth is vital. Personal interest is also significant in this decision. A niche that aligns with the affiliate's passions or expertise ensures sustainability and adds authenticity and depth to its content, greatly boosting audience engagement.

Researching and validating niche ideas is both an art and a science, requiring a blend of creativity, analytical thinking, and strategic use of tools. Keyword research tools, for instance, offer quantitative insights into the volume and competition level of terms related to the niche, providing a snapshot of market demand and saturation. On the other hand, social listening tools qualitatively assess the conversations and sentiments surrounding niche topics across social media platforms and forums, offering clues about audience interests and emerging trends. Combining quantitative data with qualitative insights, this dual approach ensures a holistic understanding of the niche's viability.

Moreover, analyzing the content within the niche offers valuable insights into audience preferences, revealing opportunities for new affiliates to address unmet needs. This comprehensive approach to research lays the groundwork for niche selection informed not by guesswork but by data and strategic analysis.

In the expansive universe of affiliate marketing, certain niches have consistently shown profitability, illustrating the importance of choosing niches strategically. Take health and wellness, for instance—it remains a popular choice due to its broad appeal and lasting relevance, making it a profitable area for affiliates. Within this broad category, sub-niches like mental health, fitness, and nutritional supplements allow affiliates to specialize further, catering to specific audience segments with customized content and product suggestions. Similarly, the technology niche, covering everything from gadgets to software, offers a dynamic market with a continuous flow of new products, driving interest and sales. Personal finance is another strong niche, addressing fundamental life aspects like budgeting, investing, and financial planning.

Each of these niches showcases the potential for profitability when chosen wisely, considering factors like market demand, competition, and personal interest. Choosing a niche is a pivotal decision in an affiliate's journey, influencing every subsequent step. It requires a strategic approach backed by thorough market analysis and a keen eye on personal interests. This decision's power lies in focusing efforts, boosting audience engagement, and maximizing earnings. Through careful evaluation using comprehensive research methods, affiliates can pinpoint niches ripe for growth, setting the stage for a thriving long-term affiliate marketing venture.

3.3 CHOOSING THE RIGHT AFFILIATE PROGRAMS AND PRODUCTS

Selecting affiliate programs and products isn't just about choosing —it's about strategically aligning with your digital identity. This alignment, fundamental for building trust and boosting sales, requires a thoughtful strategy. It involves aligning your knowledge of your niche and audience with the offerings of potential affiliate programs. The connection between your content and the products you promote is essential for keeping your audience engaged and loyal. Therefore, when selecting affiliate programs, looking beyond surface appeal is important. Consider factors like how relevant the program is to your audience, the commission rates, and the quality of the products being promoted.

Program Selection Criteria

The criteria for choosing affiliate programs are diverse, but the most important factor is how well the program fits your niche. This fit ensures that promoting products feels natural within your content, keeping it authentic and appealing to your audience. Additionally, the reputation of the affiliate program and its parent company plays a significant role in how trustworthy the promoted products are perceived. Programs affiliated with reputable companies known for quality, good customer service, and ethical practices can boost your credibility as an affiliate. Support from affiliate programs is also crucial, including access to promotional materials, product training, and helpful affiliate managers. These resources give affiliates the tools and knowledge they need to promote products effectively.

Product Relevance

A successful affiliate marketing strategy is built on promoting products that strongly connect with the audience's desires and requirements. This connection goes beyond fitting into the niche; it requires a deep understanding of the audience's challenges, goals, and the solutions for which they are searching. Products that directly tackle these aspects enhance the content and transform the affiliate from a mere promoter to a problem-solver, someone the audience trusts to give valuable advice. To ensure this relevance, thorough research and continuous interaction with the audience are necessary to understand their responses and adjust the offerings accordingly. It's an ongoing dialogue between the affiliate and their audience, where feedback guides product selection, ensuring that the promoted products continuously meet the audience's changing needs.

Commission Structures

Understanding and navigating the various commission structures found in affiliate programs is like mapping a route through a complex financial terrain. These structures come in many forms, from fixed commissions for each sale to tiered percentages based on sales volume or value. Some programs also provide recurring commissions for subscription-based products, ensuring affiliates receive ongoing income for their contributions. To choose the most beneficial commission structure, it's important to carefully evaluate the potential earnings and the level of effort required to promote the products. High-value items with lower conversion rates could offer enticing commissions but require substantial promotional work. On the other hand, products with lower prices but higher conversion rates might lead to more consistent earnings over time. This evaluation, weighing effort against potential earnings, helps affiliates select programs that best fit their content strategies and financial objectives.

Affiliate Network Benefits

When affiliates decide to join affiliate networks, they enter a domain of diverse programs offering a range of products to endorse. These networks simplify finding and managing affiliate programs, offering a centralized hub for tracking performance, handling payments, and accessing promotional resources. Besides the logistical rewards, these networks open doors to a wider selection of programs, some exclusive to the network. This access allows affiliates to explore new niches or broaden their product lineup, better catering to their audience's needs. Additionally, networks often negotiate higher commission rates for their affiliates, leveraging their collective bargaining power. The support and community within these networks, including forums, webinars, and personalized guidance, provide valuable insights and strategies to affiliates. However, the decision to join an affiliate network should be made carefully, considering the terms and conditions to ensure they align with the affiliate's goals and operational preferences.

When selecting affiliate programs and products, affiliates craft a collection of offerings that resonate with their audience and showcase their expertise. Rooted in strategic alignment and a deep understanding of audience needs, this approach transforms product promotion into an extension of content creation. It elevates the affiliate's role beyond mere marketing, positioning them as problem-solvers and trusted advisors. Through this alignment, affiliates drive conversions and cultivate loyalty, laying the groundwork for lasting success in the digital landscape.

3.4 CRAFTING YOUR UNIQUE SELLING PROPOSITION (USP)

A crucial strategy is crafting a unique selling proposition (USP) within your chosen segment of the affiliate marketing community. This proposition cuts through the noise, directing potential customers to your digital space. Your USP captures what sets your affiliate marketing apart, making it distinct and more enticing than your competitors. It's a clear declaration of value, boldly stating what your platform offers—a product and a unique experience or benefit only available through you.

Defining USP

The first step in creating this beacon is to look inward and analyze your affiliate marketing strategy to identify what makes it unique. This involves examining the products or services you promote, the content you create, and your target audience. The goal is to find that special quality that sets your platform apart. It could be your expertise in a particular niche, creative content presentation, or a strong dedication to ethical standards. It could also be your commitment to a cause, where a portion of your sales are donated to a humanitarian organization. Finding this unique aspect requires knowing your strengths, understanding the market, and recognizing any opportunities for improvement.

Alignment with Audience Values

For your USP to make a lasting impact and boost sales, it needs to mirror the values and address the wants of your intended audience. This match turns your USP from just a catchy phrase into a strong pull, drawing in customers who find their needs addressed in your offer. To make this connection work, you must keep talking to your audience and be ready to listen, learn, and adapt. This ongoing process ensures that your USP stays relevant and compelling. It's about viewing your platform as a go-between and as a gathering place where shared values and interests unite, creating a sense of community and loyalty among your audience.

Communicating Your USP

Now that you've nailed down your USP to match your audience's values, the focus shifts to communication, seamlessly integrating this proposition into all your marketing and content efforts. This requires combining your USP into the story of your platform, beyond merely repeating a slogan, making it a crucial part of how users experience it. This means everything from how your website looks to the style of your blog posts and the products you promote should highlight your unique value. Through social media, email campaigns, or the affiliate programs you choose, each interaction should consistently showcase the special advantages of picking your platform.

Evolving Your USP

Things are always changing in the fast-paced digital world—what consumers want, what's popular, and the technology itself. Because of this, your unique selling proposition (USP) can't stay the same forever. It needs to adapt along with your business and your audience. This doesn't mean you're uninteresting; it shows that your platform is growing and keeping up with the times. Checking your USP regularly means looking at what your audience wants, watching market trends, and thinking about how your platform is growing. This process might lead to refining your USP or changing direction to match new trends, ensuring your platform stays unique and keeps up in the fast-changing digital world.

With so many choices online, your USP is like a guiding light for customers to find you in the crowd. It's about showing what makes you special, what you promise, and how well you understand your audience. By clearly defining, sharing, and sometimes updating your USP, you create a clear identity in the digital market and build trust and loyalty with your audience. This whole process, which starts with thinking about your strategy and staying in touch with your audience, ensures that your affiliate marketing hits home, leading to more sales and lasting relationships.

Moving past the basics of building a strong base in our niche and creating a unique selling point, we now focus on the practical steps to make our affiliate marketing plans a reality. In the upcoming sections, we'll cover how to start your affiliate marketing venture, use digital tools effectively, and create content that captures attention and drives sales. Our goal is to give you the tools for success and encourage you to think creatively so your affiliate marketing business survives and makes a meaningful difference.

SETTING UP YOUR AFFILIATE MARKETING BUSINESS: A BLUEPRINT FOR SUCCESS

Creating an affiliate marketing business in the expansive digital world of endless possibilities requires transforming ideas into a detailed plan. Like constructing a house, every affiliate marketer needs a strong base, reliable structure, and protection against challenges. This chapter provides the essential steps to begin your affiliate marketing adventure, covering everything from legal considerations to setting up your online presence, guaranteeing that your business starts and thrives.

4.1 SETTING UP YOUR AFFILIATE MARKETING BUSINESS: A STEP-BY-STEP GUIDE

Business Structure

When starting an affiliate marketing venture, one of the first decisions is about the business structure, which is as crucial as choosing the type of building for your home. There are several options: sole proprietorship, partnership, limited liability company (LLC), and corporation, each impacting taxes, liability, and operational freedom. A sole proprietorship is simple and gives you direct control, like living in a small studio—it's easy to handle but offers little protection in legal conflicts. On the other hand, LLCs and corporations act like insurance for your home, shielding personal assets from business debts. This decision is complex, balancing your entrepreneurial goals with practical considerations of liability and taxes.

Legal Considerations

Navigating the legal aspects of affiliate marketing is akin to carefully planning a construction project, ensuring every detail complies with rules and regulations. This includes obtaining necessary permits such as business registrations and understanding how your earnings affect taxes. In the United States, this often involves dealing with the Internal Revenue Service (IRS) to get an Employer Identification Number (EIN), which is necessary for tax filings and financial transactions. While it may seem bureaucratic, having an EIN is like your business's social security number.

Moreover, following the guidelines set by the Federal Trade Commission (FTC) regarding disclosures is essential for maintaining transparency with your audience. This honesty helps build trust, which is vital for the success of your affiliate marketing endeavors.

Choosing a Domain Name

Choosing a domain name for your affiliate website is momentous, much like naming a new baby. It should reflect your niche, be memorable, and be easy to type. For instance, if your website specializes in mystery novels, a name like "MysteryManor.com" would resonate well with potential visitors. Using domain name generators can spark ideas, but your choice should reflect the unique identity of your affiliate venture, making it stand out online.

Website Hosting and Platform

Once you've secured a domain name, the next step is setting up your website's infrastructure through web hosting. This service is like renting space on the internet, provided by companies similar to landlords offering digital plots for websites. You'll encounter assorted options, ranging from shared hosting, like renting an apartment—affordable and suitable for beginners—to dedicated hosting, comparable to owning a mansion—providing ample space and control but at a higher cost.

Alongside choosing hosting, selecting a platform for creating and managing your website is required. WordPress is a popular choice due to its user-friendly interface and customization capabilities. The design and functionality of your digital property depend on the platform you choose. This combination of hosting and platform lays the groundwork for your affiliate marketing endeavors, influencing factors like website speed, security, and scalability.

Step-by-Step Website Setup

The steps involved in creating a website include everything from choosing a business structure and understanding legal requirements to picking a memorable domain name and selecting suitable hosting and platform options. Technology requirements continue to evolve, and it's important to work with your website provider to understand all the current essential steps for establishing a successful online affiliate marketing venture.

The blueprint for launching an affiliate marketing business encompasses legal frameworks and digital infrastructure and creates a structured approach for entrepreneurs. It underscores the significance of making strategic decisions regarding business structures, legal compliance, domain naming, and digital property, ensuring a solid foundation for the venture. With this framework, affiliate marketers can navigate the complexities of starting their business, positioning themselves for success in the competitive digital landscape.

4.2 CREATING YOUR AFFILIATE MARKETING WEBSITE: BASICS FOR BEGINNERS

Creating an affiliate marketing website is like laying the cornerstone of a grand structure in the vast online world. It all begins with choosing a Content Management System (CMS) that is the backbone of your digital space. Your CMS choice affects how easily you can create and manage content and determines how adaptable and expandable your site will be as it evolves. Among the many CMS options available, WordPress stands out for its user-friendly interface, extensive customization features using themes and plugins, and strong community support. Its open-source nature allows for unparalleled personalization and control, making it ideal for those aiming to establish a distinct presence in affiliate marketing.

However, your website's architecture goes beyond the technical framework of your CMS. The design and user experience (UX) are like the outer layer of your digital identity, creating a first impression for visitors. Here, aesthetics and functionality combine to create an environment that seamlessly captures attention and guides users through your content. This aspect is crucial; a well-designed website, similar to an appealing storefront, encourages exploration and interaction, increasing the chances of conversion. Elements such as clear navigation, mobile-friendly design, and fast loading times are essential for effective UX design. They ensure your site is easy to access and navigate on different devices and internet speeds, meeting the expectations of today's consumers for quick and enjoyable online experiences.

Content that draws and retains visitors is at the core of your affiliate marketing website. Managing this content requires a strategy akin to organizing a library's vast collection. Categories and tags act as the shelves and labels, guiding visitors through your site's information. Regular assessments and updates ensure that your content remains relevant and reflects current trends and audience preferences, much like how a library updates its collection to meet the evolving needs of its users.

A well-organized website enhances user experience and supports SEO efforts, making it easier for search engines to analyze and index your web pages. This organization also extends to the back-end, where a clean and structured CMS dashboard facilitates efficient content management. This allows you to focus more on creating content and less on navigating through a cluttered digital workspace.

While creating your website involves both creative and technical aspects, it also entails fulfilling legal requirements and making necessary disclosures. Compliance with these legal obligations goes beyond mere regulatory adherence; it reflects a commitment to transparency and ethical conduct. In the digital realm governed by complex laws and guidelines, affiliate marketers must disclose their partnerships and the nature of their endorsements. These disclosures, far from being bureaucratic formalities, are markers of trust and credibility. They educate visitors about the commercial relationships influencing the content, empowering them to make informed decisions. Crafting these disclosures requires a delicate balance, ensuring they are visible without being intrusive and integrated into the content in a way that respects the user's experience and intelligence.

Additionally, meeting legal requirements extends to safeguarding data and privacy, which is increasingly scrutinized in our interconnected digital world. Following regulations like the GDPR in Europe or the CCPA in California means having a clear privacy policy that outlines how visitor data is collected, used, and protected. This policy, combined with proactive measures to secure data, strengthens visitors' trust in your website. It transforms your site into a source of information and a protector of consumer rights and privacy.

These foundational aspects—choosing the right CMS, focusing on design and user experience, managing content effectively, and ensuring legal compliance—lay the groundwork for a successful online presence when building your affiliate marketing website. They determine how well your website functions and what values it upholds, influencing how visitors perceive and interact with your content. When these elements are aligned thoughtfully, your website transforms from a mere digital space into a lively community hub, attracting repeat visitors who appreciate its unique value and experience.

4.3 SEO BASICS FOR AFFILIATE MARKETERS: INCREASING YOUR SITE'S VISIBILITY

Understanding SEO

Digital marketing, SEO, or search engine optimization is crucial in directing traffic to your website, acting as a guiding light in the quest for online visibility and engagement. It functions based on algorithms that decide how high your website appears on search engine results pages (SERPs), with higher rankings leading to more visibility and, consequently, more visitors. For affiliate marketers, SEO is a tool and a fundamental strategy deeply integrated into digital success. It involves shaping your website and its content in a way that appeals not only to your audience but also to search engines, which act as gatekeepers to your digital space. The essence of SEO lies in comprehending and leveraging the criteria search engines use to rank websites, from the relevance and quality of content to user experience and the website's authority in its niche.

On-page SEO Strategies

On-page SEO focuses on enhancing specific pages on your website to improve their ranking and attract relevant traffic from search engines. This strategy involves fine-tuning various elements within your pages, such as titles, headings, content, and images, aligning them with specific keywords and phrases your target audience uses in online searches. Selecting these keywords is vital and requires a deep understanding of your audience's language and search habits as well as identifying popular terms and niche phrases that can tap into undiscovered markets. Besides keywords, on-page SEO emphasizes the importance of content quality and structure. Each piece of content should deliver value, address queries, solve problems, or offer insights, all while being presented in a format that search engines can easily understand. This includes organizing content with headers, using internal links to guide visitors through your website, and optimizing images with alt tags that describe their content. On-page SEO is about crafting a digital story that appeals to human readers and algorithmic assessments, ensuring your pages shine amidst the crowded digital landscape.

Off-page SEO Tactics

While on-page SEO deals with optimizing elements within your website, off-page SEO extends into the broader online environment to boost your site's authority through backlinks. These backlinks, originating from reputable websites and leading back to yours, function as endorsements, signaling to search engines the value and credibility of your content, thereby improving its ranking. However, obtaining backlinks requires a diplomatic approach involving outreach, networking, and building content others find worthy of linking to. This could include contributing guest posts to well-regarded sites in your niche, participating in forums and online communities, or crafting shareable infographics that naturally attract backlinks. The quality of these backlinks is crucial; links from authoritative and relevant sites carry more weight, signaling to search engines the trustworthiness and significance of your website. Therefore, off-page SEO is a strategic effort that expands your influence beyond your site's boundaries, establishing connections that enhance your site's visibility and credibility digitally.

Technical SEO

Beneath the surface of content and links lies the intricate arena of technical SEO, the foundational structure that impacts how search engines crawl, index, and rank your site. This aspect of SEO focuses on the technical properties of your website's architecture to ensure it is user-friendly and accessible to users and search engine crawlers. It covers numerous factors, such as the site's loading speed, which is important for user experience and search engine rankings, and the design's mobile responsiveness, reflecting the shift towards mobile browsing habits. Furthermore, technical SEO addresses the security of your site, advocating for HTTPS encryption to safeguard user data and build trust. Sitemaps and structured data also play key roles, providing search engines with a clear map of your site's content and context to better understand its nature. Tackling these technical elements requires a detailed approach, often involving collaboration with web developers to ensure that your site's digital framework aligns with the stringent standards set by search engines. Technical SEO is the cornerstone for the visibility and effectiveness of your affiliate marketing site, ensuring that the technical aspects of web architecture support, rather than hinder, your SEO objectives.

4.4 CONTENT IS KING: DEVELOPING YOUR CONTENT STRATEGY

Creating content that emotionally connects with your audience and aligns with your niche requires a thoughtful approach, much like a chef crafting a menu for a gourmet meal. Every content, whether a blog post, video, or social media update, should have a clear purpose—to satisfy your audience's interests while enticing them to delve deeper into your offerings. Start by outlining a content calendar that reflects important dates, trends in your niche, and what your audience finds compelling. This calendar serves as a framework, giving your content strategy direction while allowing room for spontaneous creativity or timely topics. It's important to identify the questions your audience is asking and the problems they need solutions for. By addressing these directly in your content, you position yourself as a valuable source of information, transforming casual visitors into loyal followers.

You'll find a diverse range of different content types, each format offering unique advantages. Blog posts and articles, for example, enable in-depth exploration of subjects, showcasing your expertise and boosting your site's visibility on search engines. Videos cater to the rising preference for visual content, providing an engaging way to connect with users and convey complex information effectively. Infographics condense information into visually appealing graphics, ideal for sharing on social media platforms. Podcasts create opportunities for deeper conversations, establishing a personal bond with your audience through the power of spoken words. Each content type plays a role in your strategy, attracting various audience segments and guiding them from initial awareness to taking action.

Crafting compelling content that captures attention, educates, and encourages sharing among your audience hinges on several key factors. First, maintaining authenticity in your voice and message is crucial—it builds trust and relatability, allowing your audience to feel a genuine connection to you or your brand. Second, your content should be driven by value, addressing the needs and interests of your audience to ensure its relevance and usefulness. Incorporating storytelling elements can breathe life into even the most mundane topics, transforming them into engaging narratives that leave a lasting impact on your audience. Visual elements are vital in enhancing your content by breaking up text, illustrating key points, and making it more shareable across different platforms. Lastly, including a clear and compelling call to action in each piece of content guides your audience on what actions to take next, whether signing up for a newsletter, purchasing, or sharing your content with others.

Promoting your content across various channels is essential for expanding its reach and driving traffic to your website. Social media platforms offer direct access to your audience, facilitating real-time engagement and feedback. Tailoring your content to fit each platform's unique format and audience is key, from concise and impactful posts on Twitter to visually appealing stories on Instagram. Email marketing remains a potent tool for reaching your audience directly in their inboxes, allowing for personalized messages to boost engagement and conversions. Consider segmenting your email list to deliver more tailored content, increase relevance, and improve response rates. Furthermore, collaborating with others and seeking guest posting opportunities can introduce your content to new audiences, expanding your reach. Continuously evaluating and analyzing your promotional efforts is vital—it helps you refine your strategies and focus on the channels that yield the best results.

Content creation and promotion are at the core of a winning strategy. Crafting content that suits your audience's needs and creating materials that educate, engage, and inspire are crucial steps in building your online presence. By using different types of content and promoting strategically, you capture your audience's interest and encourage meaningful interactions, forming a community of loyal followers who trust and value your insights.

As we conclude this exploration of content strategy, keep in mind the power of well-crafted content. It acts as a magnet, drawing your audience in, fostering connections that turn casual visitors into dedicated followers, and propelling your affiliate marketing efforts forward. Every piece of content tells your brand's story, creating a narrative that resonates deeply with your audience and lasts over time. Let's carry these principles forward, transforming our digital platforms into engaging and conversion-driven masterpieces.

MASTERING THE SOCIAL SPHERE: AMPLIFYING YOUR AFFILIATE REACH

In today's digital era, social media stands out as the primary arena for affiliate marketing. It's like a bustling marketplace where interactions happen, trends emerge, and brands forge personal connections with their followers. Picture a lively market square filled with traders and customers, each stall showcasing its products uniquely. Social media mirrors this dynamic environment online, providing affiliate marketers a stage to display their offerings and interact directly with their audience. Here, content gets viewed, shared, liked, commented on, and becomes part of broader discussions. With the right approach, affiliate marketers can leverage this active platform to convert followers into customers and transform social media posts into revenue.

5.1 THE ROLE OF SOCIAL MEDIA IN YOUR AFFILIATE STRATEGY

Choosing Platforms

Choosing the right social media platforms is like picking the perfect spot for your market stall. Each platform attracts a specific audience and encourages a unique type of interaction. Instagram, known for its visual content, appeals to a younger crowd focused on images, making it great for lifestyle and beauty affiliates. On the other hand, LinkedIn caters to professionals, making it suitable for business, tech, or education affiliates. Twitter thrives on instant engagement, making it a go-to for affiliates who love trending topics and discussions. The key is identifying where your target audience hangs out and tailoring your content accordingly. This strategic decision ensures that your posts reach the right people, increasing your chances of engagement and conversions.

Content Variety

In social media, content is crucial, but diversity keeps things interesting. Posting only promotional content can bore your followers, prompting them to look for more engaging content elsewhere. It's essential to strike a balance. Mix educational content that teaches or solves problems, entertaining posts that spark joy or provoke thoughts and promotional content that subtly features your affiliate products. For example, a cooking affiliate might share recipe videos (educational), stories about kitchen mishaps (entertaining), and posts showcasing favorite kitchen tools (promotional). This variety showcases the affiliate's expertise and caters to different interests within their audience, making the feed dynamic and engaging.

Community Engagement

Social media is about creating communities—groups of people sharing common interests, beliefs, or goals. Building these communities can turn passive followers into active participants for affiliates. Engaging with your audience by responding to comments, starting conversations, and providing opportunities for followers to share their thoughts and experiences makes your social media presence more interactive. Hosting live Q&A sessions regularly, for example, allows followers to ask questions, give feedback, and feel like they're part of the conversation. This kind of engagement helps you build a relationship with your audience, leading to trust and loyalty that can boost the effectiveness of your affiliate promotions.

Influencer Collaborations

In the expansive world of social media, influencers function as guides, directing followers toward products and experiences that resonate. Collaborating with influencers in your niche expands your reach by tapping into their engaged and trusting audience. The key to successful partnerships lies in alignment—not just in niche but also in values and audience demographics. For instance, teaming up with an influencer known for promoting sustainability can be a great match for affiliates who promote eco-friendly products. When done authentically, these collaborations can add credibility to your affiliate offerings and introduce your brand to a wider audience, increasing your visibility and impact.

Social Media Strategy Checklists

A checklist is a handy tool for affiliates, ensuring they cover all the important aspects of their social media strategy. Creating good daily, weekly, and monthly checklists provides a step-by-step guide to make the most of your social media presence, covering everything from choosing the right platforms and planning diverse content to engaging with your community and collaborating with influencers. It serves as a roadmap, helping affiliates confidently navigate the busy world of social media and transform their digital presence into a lively hub of interaction and conversion.

With rapid changes in the dynamic social media world, checklist requirements may shift. Research examples of social media checklists regularly to ensure new elements are considered. The most important activity to include on a daily checklist is reviewing and responding to comments and messages and monitoring mentions of your brand on every platform. Timely communication and connection with your audience is essential. Most consumers expect a reply within 24 hours. You should also check trending topics and products and connect with other brands and individuals to build relationships. Remember, content is key. Your daily checklist should include updating content, scheduling posts for the next day, removing outdated information, and ensuring posted content does not suffer from technology glitches, such as posted videos that won't play or broken links.

Your weekly social media checklist includes creating content and scheduling when it should be posted. Research what your competitors are doing to determine if you should shift your strategy. Evaluate weekly goals and brainstorm new ideas and strategies to meet or exceed these targets. Evaluate performance metrics and build upon your successes. The weekly checklist should also include personal development to keep your skills and knowledge up to date. This includes learning about new social media platforms, testing new content development tool features, understanding legal and regulatory changes, and exploring other ways to keep your affiliate marketing business on the cutting edge.

A monthly checklist focuses heavily on analytics and auditing. Checking analytics provides a big-picture perspective of how your business is performing. Evaluate trends with your targeted audience to ensure you continually meet their interests and needs. Analyze your social profiles to ensure they are consistent and current. Adjust your social media strategy to directly align with marketing goals. Refine or set new goals to adjust this strategy based on what you learned about the previous month.

Affiliates can connect, engage, and influence on social media. With its various platforms and diverse audiences, social media offers creativity, engagement, and promotion opportunities. By strategically selecting platforms, creating diverse content, fostering community engagement, and partnering with influencers, affiliates can expand their reach, making social media a powerful tool for growth and success.

5.2 THE PSYCHOLOGY BEHIND EFFECTIVE CONTENT

Understanding the intricate workings of psychological triggers that drive purchases is like discovering a treasure trove of strategies to engage audiences for affiliate marketers. Buyers' actions are motivated by a complex blend of needs, wants, dreams, and self-image. To incorporate these triggers into your content effectively, you need a deep understanding of your audience's thoughts and a thorough exploration of the emotions and logic influencing their decisions. This process starts by pinpointing their challenges and desires and linking them to the solutions or experiences offered by your affiliate products. By framing your content around these solutions, you shift your storytelling from mere product showcasing to providing compelling answers to your audience's most significant concerns.

Using storytelling effectively becomes a strong way to build emotional ties, turning product suggestions into stories that strike a personal chord. The skill lies in creating entertaining stories that include your products in situations people can relate to, making them an important part of the story's ending. This might mean sharing personal experiences with a product, showing how it helps overcome difficulties or reach objectives or including user testimonials in a broader story of change and achievement. These stories make your content feel genuine and relatable, encouraging people to connect with your products emotionally and gently nudging them toward purchasing.

Social proof is like a solid building block of trust and influence, tapping into our natural tendency to look for approval from others before making choices. Incorporating reviews, testimonials, and case studies into your content is a strong endorsement, showing real-life examples of people being satisfied with the products you promote. This boosts your credibility and gives concrete proof of how valuable and effective your products are; it makes sense for potential buyers to want to make a purchase. Additionally, sharing stories of how your products have solved problems or improved lives adds a layer of relatability, helping potential customers see themselves benefiting similarly.

Personalizing your content means tailoring your message to fit the specific needs, interests, and desires of different groups within your audience, ensuring your message feels personalized and relevant to each individual. This approach requires a deep understanding of your audience, categorizing them based on age, behavior, preferences, and where they are in their journey as potential buyers. Personalized content could involve creating customized email campaigns that speak to specific interests, adjusting social media posts for different audience segments, or suggesting products based on each user's past interactions. By making your content feel unique to each person, you increase its relevance and show that you understand and care about their needs, strengthening your connection with your audience and boosting the chances of them making a purchase.

Affiliate marketers open doors to a space where engagement, trust, and conversion come together by understanding the psychological elements that make content compelling. By delving into why people buy things, crafting stories that people can relate to, using social proof, and customizing content, you create a landscape full of opportunities to connect and influence. This thoughtful approach to creating content goes beyond simple promotion; it turns your affiliate offerings into stories of overcoming challenges, change, and satisfaction. Every piece of content plays a part in your audience's journey in this space, helping them make choices that meet their needs and align with their hopes and identities.

5.3 CRAFTING HIGH-CONVERTING AFFILIATE CONTENT

Creating content that grabs attention and motivates people to act is like finding a hidden route to successful sales. Although challenging, this task relies on a fundamental principle of providing real value. Affiliate marketers pack useful information and persuasive elements with every sentence and article, constructing a story that draws readers in by addressing their needs and solving their problems. This focus on value, beyond just showcasing products, builds a bond of trust and mutual benefit, turning reader engagement into a journey toward fulfilling their desires.

Placing calls-to-action (CTAs) strategically within this narrative is crucial, as signposts that gently guide readers from interest to making a decision. These carefully placed and well-crafted CTAs don't disrupt the flow of the content; they fit naturally into the story, suggesting the next steps almost as if the reader thought of them themselves. Whether prompting readers to learn more, watch a tutorial, or take advantage of a special offer, each CTA subtly encourages progress toward conversion without being pushy, striking a balance between guidance and independence.

Integrating product mentions and recommendations into content requires skill to ensure they enhance rather than detract from the value provided. This integration isn't forceful but a subtle skill where products naturally fit into the story as solutions, making their relevance clear. Here, the affiliate marketer becomes a trusted advisor whose suggestions naturally arise from the discussion, and their recommendations carry genuine endorsement. This not only boosts the authenticity of the content but also increases its persuasive impact, as products are directly linked to fulfilling the audience's needs and desires.

Measuring the success of affiliate content adds a quantitative aspect to this creative process, providing insights into the effectiveness of strategies and how well the narratives resonate. Conversion rates and affiliate income are key metrics here, showing how well content turns engagement into action. Yet, beyond these numbers, understanding the audience's interactions and feedback offers clues for refining content strategies. Beyond crunching numbers, this ongoing assessment and improvement process creates engagement through a dynamic conversation with the audience. Data guides adjustments and innovations to boost relevance, engagement, and conversion. Through this continuous cycle, the affiliate marketer hone their skills, refining content focus and improving their ability to guide the audience toward beneficial decisions.

Navigating affiliate marketing's complexities means creating high-impact content which requires a mix of strategic thinking, creative finesse, and analytical skills. Central to this challenge is the commitment to delivering value. This principle shapes every aspect of content creation, from integrating calls-to-action and product recommendations to evaluating and enhancing performance. This dedication ensures content isn't just a tool for promotion but a means to build trust, foster engagement, and guide the audience toward informed choices. By following this approach, the affiliate marketer crafts content and experiences that turn value into action, transforming digital spaces into places where meaningful narratives drive conversions.

5.4 BLOGGING SUCCESS: TIPS AND TRICKS FOR AFFILIATE MARKETERS

Blogging is a powerful tool for affiliate marketers in digital storytelling and influence, shedding light on paths that lead to enlightenment and engagement. This digital medium blends information and persuasion, and requires a careful approach, where consistency, SEO optimization, engaging formats, and strategic partnerships create a dynamic array of content. When executed skillfully, these components captivate audiences and navigate them through the intricate landscape of affiliate marketing, transforming curiosity into action.

Consistency is Key

Consistency plays a vital role in this endeavor. Mastering the delicate balance of content creation demands a dedicated commitment to posting regularly. This commitment is the cornerstone of an effective blogging strategy, ensuring a steady stream of content that keeps audience interest alive and encourages them to return for more. Imagine the delight of readers as they uncover fresh insights each time they visit, strengthening their connection with your blog.

This reliability becomes an implicit promise of value, acting as a magnet that draws visitors back, turning brief interactions into enduring relationships. Achieving this requires careful planning, aligning posts with thematic series or industry trends, creating an editorial calendar to guide your blogging journey, and ensuring each post serves a clear purpose.

SEO-rich Content

Visibility is key to success in a digital landscape. Incorporating SEO best practices into your blogging efforts is a crucial strategy that must not be underestimated. Going beyond simply adding keywords, visibility involves a thorough examination of how your posts are structured to ensure they are not just easy to find but also easy for search engines to understand and categorize. Crafting titles that grab attention while summarizing your post's main idea, creating meta descriptions that intrigue readers and encourage clicks, and using header tags to organize your content for both readability and SEO effectiveness are crucial. Additionally, using tools to monitor keyword performance and staying updated on algorithm changes helps keep your content aligned with the evolving standards of search engines. This careful optimization turns your blog into a guiding light amid the digital landscape, allowing search engines and readers to navigate its content effectively.

Engaging Formats

The digital world is like a creative playground of diverse content types, allowing for experimentation and fresh ideas. Adding variety to your blogging formats breathes excitement into your content plan, giving readers a range of perspectives and styles. How-to guides offering solutions to problems add value and establish your expertise in your field. Honest and detailed product reviews and comparisons help readers make informed choices, giving them clarity and confidence. Personal stories and case studies, where you share vulnerabilities alongside lessons, connect with readers personally, bridging the gap between digital content and human experience. This mix enriches the reader's journey and caters to the preferences of different audience segments, ensuring your blog remains lively and engaging.

Guest Blogging

Expanding your online presence through guest blogging opens doors to new audiences and strengthens your blog's authority with backlinks. This strategic partnership introduces your insights to communities that may have yet to discover your blog. Choosing the right platforms for guest posts involves carefully considering values, audience fit, and content quality. Making guest posts that resonate with the host blog's audience while enticing them to explore your blog requires providing value and sparking curiosity. Moreover, guest blogging boosts your blog's SEO standing by creating a backlink network that enhances your site's credibility and search engine ranking. When done effectively, this collaborative approach transforms your blog from an individual platform into a well-connected entity in the digital realm.

Adopting these core strategies becomes essential in the complex world of blogging in affiliate marketing, where words can inform, persuade, and convert. Consistency in posting, optimizing for search engines, exploring diverse content formats, and strategically pursuing guest blogging opportunities combine to form a strong blogging strategy. Through these tactics, affiliate marketers engage and retain their audiences and establish their influence online, making blogs valuable hubs of information, interaction, and action.

5.5 LEVERAGING VIDEO CONTENT IN AFFILIATE MARKETING

Videos are a powerful tool for engaging audiences, breaking communication barriers, and building direct connections. This medium offers affiliate marketers a dynamic platform to tell stories, demonstrate products, and persuade viewers. However, using video effectively requires careful planning based on different platforms' unique characteristics, audiences, and content preferences. YouTube, known for its depth and educational content, is a major player. At the same time, shorter videos on social media platforms like Instagram and Facebook cater to audiences looking for quick, engaging content. Choosing the right platform depends on the affiliate campaign's content type, audience preferences, and strategic goals, ensuring maximum visibility and engagement.

Understanding video SEO adds complexity to this process, as it involves optimizing videos for search engines and platform searches. This starts with keyword research to find terms that relate to the target audience, incorporating these keywords into video titles, descriptions, and tags to improve discoverability. Creating compelling thumbnails, using closed captions and transcripts for accessibility, and embedding videos on websites with keyword-rich introductions all contribute to SEO, increasing the chances of videos appearing in search results. This video and text content integration amplifies the impact of affiliate marketing efforts, extending their reach and effectiveness.

Video engagement strategies unfold like a story where viewers aren't just watching but actively participating. Including polls, questions, and calls-to-action in videos turn passive viewing into an interactive experience. It invites viewers to share their thoughts, preferences, and decisions, fostering community and involvement. Encouraging comments and discussions beneath videos adds to this engagement, creating a lively forum for exchange that enriches the viewer experience and provides insights for improving content. Live video sessions take this engagement up a notch, allowing direct communication and Q&A sessions, building rapport with the audience, and boosting affiliate promotions' authenticity and effectiveness.

Monitoring video performance through platform analytics reveals valuable insights into viewer behavior, preferences, and engage-ment patterns. These detailed analytics help evaluate video content effectiveness, from views and watch time to interaction rates and conversion metrics. Using this data guides content refinement, highlighting strengths to capitalize on and areas for improvement. It informs content strategy adjustments regarding topics covered, presentation style, or calls to action, ensuring each video is optimized for performance and impact. Continuously analyzing video analytics creates a cycle of learning and adapta-tion, where data informs strategy and shapes future content, leading to progressive improvements in affiliate marketing outcomes.

In affiliate marketing, video content is like a conductor's baton, orchestrating engagement by combining platform choices, video

SEO, engagement strategies, and analytics. This approach blends strategy with creativity, using data to make informed decisions and create impactful content that resonates with audiences and drives conversions. Video is more than just content; it's an immersive experience that captivates, educates, and motivates action, making it a vital tool for affiliate marketers.

5.6 EMAIL MARKETING: THE UNTAPPED GOLDMINE FOR AFFILIATES

Email marketing is a hidden gem within digital marketing strategies. It plays a pivotal role in affiliate marketing by turning passive visitors into active customers. It's a personalized approach beyond the impersonal nature of broader digital interactions, nurturing leads and building relationships. To make it work, you must carefully build, segment, automate, and analyze your email list, creating messages that resonate with your audience.

Building a List

The first step in effective email marketing is creating a list of people interested in your niche or products. This involves strategically placing sign-up prompts across your online platforms and enticing visitors with exclusive content or discounts to encourage them to share their email addresses. Creating these offers requires understanding your audience's desires and what motivates them to engage further, turning casual interest into dedicated subscribers.

Segmentation and Personalization

As your email list grows, the focus shifts from gathering contacts to strategic segmentation—dividing your list into groups based on demographics, behavior, or specific interests. This division allows you to customize email content, ensuring messages are relevant to each group's unique preferences. Personalization takes this further by addressing recipients by name, mentioning previous interactions, or tailoring content to their behaviors or milestones. This personalized approach increases the perceived value of each email, turning generic messages into personalized conversations and fostering a stronger connection with subscribers. This tailored strategy boosts engagement rates and sets the stage for higher conversion rates as recipients feel recognized, understood, and valued.

Automation and Funnels

The sophistication of email marketing shines through the strategic use of automation tools—digital tools that manage the delivery of content at specific times or in response to certain triggers. These tools enable the creation of sales funnels and carefully crafted sequences of emails that guide subscribers from initial interest to purchase. Each email in the sequence serves a distinct purpose, such as building trust, offering value, addressing concerns, or presenting offers. Developing these sequences requires a deep understanding of the customer's journey and a skillful storytelling approach to ensure each message complements the last, gently guiding the subscriber toward taking the desired action. Automation streamlines this process, ensuring the right message is delivered at the right time to maximize conversion opportunities with minimal manual effort.

Performance Analysis

In email marketing, hitting "send" is just the journey's beginning. Evaluating success involves analyzing metrics such as open rates, click-through rates, and conversions. This analysis gives insight into what works well with your audience and what doesn't. Regularly reviewing these metrics allows for refining your email marketing strategies and finding areas to improve and innovate. Monitoring the performance of individual emails and sequences in your sales funnels shows trends and preferences, guiding adjustments in content, timing, and audience segmentation. This ongoing process ensures your email marketing stays dynamic, adapting to your subscribers' changing needs and behaviors while aligning with your overall affiliate marketing objectives.

Email marketing stands out in affiliate marketing as a tool for personalized engagement, offering a direct connection to your audience amidst digital noise. This strategy, centered on building lists, segmenting audiences, automating workflows, and analyzing performance, turns emails into powerful tools for conversion and building loyalty. Crafting relevant, personalized content delivered strategically helps nurture leads, guiding them to informed decisions that benefit them and you. Email marketing is a crucial part of a complete affiliate marketing strategy, forging connections beyond the inbox and strengthening relationships with your brand.

5.7 OVERCOMING CONTENT CREATION CHALLENGES

Navigating the world of content creation in affiliate marketing requires steering through a constantly changing and sometimes unpredictable landscape. There are many challenges, from coming up with new ideas to managing the practical aspects of bringing those ideas to life while maintaining high creativity and consistency. Overcoming these challenges requires creativity, planning, and resilience to ensure your content remains top-notch despite production pressures.

Content Ideation (Generating Ideas)

The foundation of great content lies in the creative process which blends curiosity, research, and turning insights into actionable concepts. However, this process isn't always straightforward. Sometimes, there's a shortage of fresh and relevant themes that will hit home with your audience. To combat this, it's key to establish a routine of exploring systematically. This means staying updated with industry news, participating in community discussions, and staying aware of emerging trends. Tools like content idea generators and social listening platforms can also help spark new ideas. Beyond tools, maintaining a mindset of curiosity, where every interaction and question can lead to new content ideas, ensures a continuous flow of creativity.

Resource Allocation

Effectively managing time and resources for content creation while maintaining quality is a delicate balance. It requires a realistic assessment of your capabilities compared to your goals, leading to a practical approach to content production. One strategy is prioritizing content types based on their potential impact and resource requirements. This might involve focusing on high-engagement formats while streamlining or automating others. Content calendars and project management tools can help visualize your content pipeline and evenly distribute the workload. Additionally, batching—dedicating focused time blocks to similar tasks—can streamline the content creation, making it more efficient without compromising quality or depth.

Scaling Content

Producing more content, reaching a larger audience, and boosting engagement typically require additional time and personal capacity. Exploring collaboration and ways to multiply content helps overcome these obstacles. Outsourcing some content tasks to freelancers or agencies can bring fresh perspectives and save time for strategic planning. Also, involving guest contributors brings diverse voices to your platform and expands your reach. Repurposing content is another effective strategy—converting one piece into different formats to maximize its usefulness and visibility. For instance, a webinar can become a blog post, an infographic, and several social media posts, each targeting different segments of your audience. Scaling content this way broadens its impact and reinforces key messages across various platforms.

Creative Burnout

Creative burnout is one of the toughest challenges in content creation, where inspiration diminishes, and ideas need improvement. Overcoming burnout requires recognizing creativity as a renewable resource that needs rest and breaks. Regular rest periods and disconnecting help create mental space for new ideas to surface. Seeking inspiration from diverse sources like nature, art, or different fields of knowledge can reignite creativity. Also, trying out various types of content can refresh your perspective and reignite your passion. By adopting these strategies deliberately, creative burnout can be a temporary setback rather than a long-term problem.

Navigating the Challenges

Successfully navigating content creation challenges in affiliate marketing involves a comprehensive and adaptable approach. Do not become discouraged! Each challenge presents an opportunity for growth—from sparking creativity to managing resources effectively, scaling content production, and preventing burnout. By tackling these hurdles with creativity and resilience, you establish your presence in the affiliate marketing landscape, guaranteeing your content is relatable to your audience, drives engagement, and builds lasting connections.

MAKE A DIFFERENCE WITH YOUR REVIEW

Audience reviews are an important part of driving traffic to your business. Every single review can greatly influence this process. Reviewing something that might seem like a small task, but it can change people's minds, shape how they see things, and help them make purchasing choices.

This is especially true for your review of "Affiliate Marketing for Beginners: Unlock Online Income, Avoid Costly Mistakes & Pitfalls, Create a Solid Foundation for Long-Term Success, and Achieve Financial Independence" by Audrey K Andado. Your review allows you to share your experience with the book, which then serves as a resource for others seeking to navigate the challenges of affiliate marketing.

Unlock the Power of Generosity

By sharing your insights and reflections, you're helping those who are uncertain find their direction. Your review isn't just about writing down your thoughts; it's a way of offering support and guidance to others in the same situation you once were. It's like building a bridge between your experience and the hopes of others, giving them the clarity and courage to move forward.

Please share your thoughts on the book. Did it shed light on things you didn't understand? Did it clear up any misconceptions you had about affiliate marketing? How has your viewpoint changed, and what actions are you now ready to take? Your story, shaped by your experiences and insights, adds richness and understanding to the knowledge of future readers.

Below is the Amazon review page for "Affiliate Marketing for Beginners" by Audrey K Andado. I eagerly await your review, reflecting on your journey through the book. Let your words guide others as they navigate affiliate marketing.

Please follow these links to the book review page, where your experiences and thoughts can guide others. Your review isn't just about giving feedback; it's a way to show the path you've traveled, a beacon of wisdom for those coming after you.

STRATEGIC CONTENT MASTERY: ORCHESTRATING YOUR AFFILIATE MARKETING SYMPHONY

Creating content is like orchestrating a complex symphony. Each piece, whether it's a blog post or a social media update, plays a unique role in captivating, educating, and convincing your audience. To conduct this symphony effectively, you need a content calendar. This tool organizes your content strategy, ensuring that each piece reaches your audience at the right time and with the right message.

6.1 CREATING A CONTENT CALENDAR: PLANNING FOR SUCCESS

Strategic Planning

Imagine going on a long road trip without a map or plan. You might face unexpected obstacles, miss important landmarks, or end up far from your destination without enough resources. Similarly, navigating affiliate marketing without a content calendar can be uncertain and inefficient. A content calendar is your strategic guide, proactively mapping out your posts, promotions, and product launches in advance. It aligns with important dates, tracks audience trends, and supports your marketing goals. This foresight allows you to create high-quality content that meets your audience's needs while taking advantage of timely opportunities.

Content Themes

Just as a chef plans a menu to offer a mix of flavors and coherence, organizing themes or series in your content strategy keeps your audience interested and establishes your expertise in your niche. These themes create a storyline for your audience to follow, giving them a reason to return for more. For example, a monthly theme focusing on sustainable living might include blog posts about eco-friendly products, social media challenges encouraging followers to share their green habits, and email newsletters discussing the environmental impact of consumer choices. Themes can focus on seasonal or holiday celebrations, such as Earth Day. These themes build anticipation, deepen audience engagement, and strengthen their connection to your content and the affiliate products you endorse.

Flexibility

Being adaptable is key when using a content calendar. It should give structure without being so strict that it hinders creativity or stops you from responding to unexpected events. Flexibility means you can adjust your content strategy quickly if market trends change, new products emerge, or your audience gives feedback. This ability to adapt is necessary for staying relevant and connected to your audience. For instance, if a new product launches in your niche and gets a lot of attention, you can tweak your content calendar to feature reviews or guides about that product, taking advantage of the excitement to boost traffic and engagement.

Collaboration and Delegation

Working together and sharing tasks is extremely important in content creation. Like an orchestra needs all its musicians, effective content creation often involves teamwork. A shared content calendar helps by showing what content is coming up, when it's due, and who's responsible for each task. This visibility lets team members contribute their writing, design, or analytics skills, ensuring each piece of content benefits from different perspectives. You can also plan guest posts or collaborations with influencers and fit them into your calendar, bringing new voices into your content and reaching new audiences.

Research different social media content planning calendars and adopt best practices that most closely align with your business's needs. In the ever-changing affiliate marketing world, these calendars will evolve to include new technologies and content types. Create a template for an interactive content calendar to help you implement these ideas. This digital tool lets you visually map your content strategy, including posts, themes, and promotions across various channels. The template should be flexible, allowing you to adjust it according to your needs and objectives. It should include sections for content type, channel, team member responsibility, status, and notes, providing flexibility and fostering collaboration. This interactive calendar functions as both a planning tool and a dynamic document that adapts as your strategy evolves, promoting continuous engagement and improvement of your content plan.

By utilizing a content calendar in your affiliate marketing efforts, you can coordinate your actions effectively, ensuring that each piece of content connects with your audience. This chapter establishes a structured yet adaptable approach to content strategy, anticipating audience needs, utilizing thematic storytelling, and encouraging collaboration. With these methods, your content can reach its target audience effectively, creating engagement, establishing expertise, and setting the stage for successful ventures in affiliate marketing.

6.2 FINANCIAL PLANNING AND MANAGEMENT FOR AFFILIATES

Managing financial resources carefully is necessary for the long-term growth and operational strength of your affiliate marketing business. This process is more than just handling paperwork; it requires strategic planning to foresee future needs, allocate funds wisely, and establish a robust system for monitoring, analyzing, and ensuring compliance.

Budgeting for Growth

Budgeting to expand balances immediate needs against future investments. Reinvesting in content, a key part of affiliate marketing requires funds and a vision for how content can evolve to engage and convert audiences. Paid advertising also needs a strategic budget to maximize returns while aligning with organic growth efforts. Investing in technology, like analytics tools and automation software, supports efficiency, deeper insights, and scalable operations. This budgeting approach, guided by strategy, ensures that every dollar spent contributes to future growth and strengthens the foundation of your affiliate marketing business.

Tracking Financial Performance

Setting up systems to track income, expenses, and profitability goes beyond basic record-keeping; it becomes a strategic tool for decision-making and adapting strategies. This system acts like the nervous system of your affiliate marketing business, signaling its health, efficiency, and areas needing attention. Using accounting software designed for digital marketing aids in gaining real-time insights into financial performance. Regular reviews and analyses reveal patterns, the effectiveness of marketing strategies, the profitability of partnerships, and how efficiently expenses are allocated. These insights empower affiliate marketers to make informed decisions, optimize strategy for better returns, and sustain steady growth.

Diversifying Income Sources

To secure financial stability, avoid depending solely on one source of income. Instead, aim for a mix of revenue streams. This strategy helps reduce risks from market changes, shifts in affiliate programs, and changes in customer behavior. Joining multiple affiliate programs creates different sources of income, each with its dynamics and potential. Also, exploring other ways to earn money, like selling digital products, offering consulting services, or running membership programs, strengthens financial resilience. This diversification, aligned with your brand and audience, ensures a steady income even when market conditions change, protecting against unexpected challenges and ensuring the long-term success of your affiliate marketing efforts.

Tax Considerations and Compliance

Managing taxes and meeting legal requirements also requires careful attention and planning. Earning money through affiliate marketing means dealing with tax implications that vary depending on where you live. It is crucial to understand and follow tax laws. Identifying expenses that can be deducted, such as marketing costs or software fees, helps lower your tax bill while ensuring compliance. Consulting with a tax expert with digital marketing income is wise to avoid legal issues and provide accurate reporting. Additionally, as affiliate marketing can involve international sales, it's important to consider cross-border tax obligations and strategies to maximize post-tax income. This proactive approach to tax planning and compliance safeguards against financial and legal problems while ensuring your affiliate marketing business is financially responsible and strategically prepared for the future.

6.3 SEO FOR AFFILIATE MARKETERS: INTERMEDIATE STRATEGIES

Keyword Research Expansion

We dive deeper into keyword research to reach the right audience effectively, focusing on long-tail keywords and user intent. Long-tail keywords are specific and based on queries, revealing what your audience wants, their problems, questions, and the solutions they want. These keywords are typically phrases made from three to five words, which provide more information into specific audience needs. For example, users may search for the keyword "shoes," or they may search using the long-tail keyword phrase "Ladies athletic shoes with arch support." While they may not bring huge traffic, they attract quality visitors who are closer to making a purchase decision. This requires a detailed understanding of your audience's needs and motivations, using tools to analyze search trends and user queries for strategic content alignment.

On-page Optimization

Improving on-page elements boosts your content's visibility in search engine rankings. It goes beyond incorporating keywords into meta tags and headers; it involves optimizing every aspect to improve user experience and help search engines better comprehend and rank your content. Meta descriptions should be clear and compelling to make users want to click through from search results. Headers organize your content and show its importance, strategically placing keywords for impact. Optimizing images with descriptive alt tags and file names improves accessibility and helps search engines understand your visual content. When done correctly, this optimization increases your content's visibility, making it stand out and attracting search engines and potential customers.

Content Structure

The structure of your content needs to be visually appealing and functionally efficient. How your content is organized affects how users navigate and understand it and influences how search engines rank your pages. A clear structure with logical headings and a smooth flow of ideas makes it easy for users to find information and stay engaged, reducing bounce rates. Incorporating strategic keywords in headings and throughout the text helps with SEO, making your content more relevant and easier to find. Using structured data markup can enhance visibility by assisting search engines in showcasing rich snippets within search results. Organizing your content meticulously based on user behavior and search engine guidelines ensures that your affiliate marketing efforts are based on clarity, relevance, and accessibility.

Link-building

Building trust and authority using a well-thought-out link-building strategy is essential for boosting your site's credibility and ranking in search results. Quality backlinks from reputable sites enhance your site's authority and visibility. However, it extends beyond accumulating numerous links by establishing connections and generating top-notch, shareable content that naturally draws in links.

Guest posting on respected sites introduces your content to new audiences and earns valuable backlinks that show search engines your site is relevant and trustworthy. By creating outstanding content and reaching out strategically, you can enhance your site's SEO profile, making it more visible and authoritative in the digital landscape.

6.4 UTILIZING ANALYTICS TO REFINE YOUR CONTENT AND MARKETING STRATEGY

Every action, like clicks, views, and engagements, holds valuable insights, and using analytics smartly becomes important for refining strategies. This detailed and comprehensive data gives a lens into how well your content is performing and how audiences are interacting with it. Marketers can find hidden opportunities for improvement and growth by carefully studying metrics and patterns. Analytics is a guide that helps marketers align their content and strategies better with their audience's wants.

A/B testing is a prime example of how data can lead to small but impactful improvements. This method involves comparing two versions, like headlines or calls-to-action, in a controlled setup to see which performs better. The goal is to learn from these tests and make changes that make content more engaging and effective in driving conversions. This ongoing process of testing, analyzing, and tweaking enables affiliate marketers to learn which versions work best, allowing money and resources to be shifted toward optimal strategies. A/B testing is crucial for creating deeply relatable audience content, encouraging consumers to engage and take action.

Delving deeper into analytics uncovers much information about audience demographics, interests, and behaviors. This exploration requires a detailed understanding of different audience segments, including their age, location, devices they use, and more. It also involves analyzing their interests and how they interact with content. This data helps create content that addresses audience needs and desires when used correctly. Strategically targeting content based on these insights leads to higher relevance and engagement and fosters a strong connection and loyalty among the audience.

Monitoring trends in content performance provides insight into how customers change and adapt. By closely examining these trends, we can spot chances to be creative and make smart changes. We learn from how people interact with content, what they like, and what works best for different types of content and strategies. This analysis helps us plan future content in a way that meets audience needs and takes advantage of new opportunities. When we combine this trend analysis with strategic planning, we can create content that grabs attention and gets people to take action.

Competition is fierce and always changing in affiliate marketing. Using analytics intelligently helps you adapt your goals. It helps us keep improving our content and marketing tactics, so they stay relevant and interesting to our audience. We can make informed decisions by using tools like A/B testing and looking at who our audience is and how they behave. This data-driven approach ensures that everything we create isn't just made randomly but is a step toward building stronger connections and achieving success.

Analytics help us understand what's important by showing us what works and what doesn't. They guide us in refining our strategies to match what our audience wants. Looking ahead, the lessons we learn from using analytics will continue to be important in creating content that connects with people and leads to success in affiliate marketing.

SEO MASTERY: ADVANCED TECHNIQUES FOR AFFILIATE MARKETERS

Effective SEO (Search Engine Optimization) techniques help websites move forward, catching the interest of search engines and potential customers alike. Optimization requires technical skills, careful planning, and a deep understanding of search engine algorithms. This section explores advanced SEO strategies, including detailed keyword planning, optimizing website structure, advanced link-building methods, and the crucial role of technical SEO assessments.

7.1 KEYWORDS, LINKS, ARCHITECTURE, AUDITS AND STRATEGY IMPLEMENTATION

Comprehensive Keyword Strategy

A thorough keyword strategy is like having a map when you enter a library to find a specific book. Without that map or a librarian's help, you might wander through the shelves, hoping to stumble upon the right section. Similarly, keywords act as signposts, guiding search engines to your content. Advanced keyword research goes beyond basic terms, exploring longer phrases and understanding user intent. Tools like Google's Keyword Planner and SEMrush provide insights into these longer, more specific phrases that users use when they're closer to deciding or seeking detailed information. Targeting these phrases helps your content better match users' desires, increasing the chances of catching their attention at critical moments.

Site Architecture for SEO

Website structure is the blueprint for SEO success. A well-organized site helps search engines crawl and index content efficiently, like a library where books are arranged neatly for easy discovery. The site needs to have a clear hierarchy, easy navigation, and URLs that show how the site is organized. Using breadcrumb navigation helps users know where they are on the site and gives search engines more clues about its structure. For affiliate marketers, ensuring that product reviews, comparisons, and informational content are easy to find can greatly impact how well the site performs in search engine rankings.

Advanced Link Building

Getting backlinks from other websites to yours helps build relationships in a professional network. Each link is a vote of confidence from one site to another, telling search engines that the content is valuable and trustworthy. However, not all backlinks are the same. Focusing on getting high-quality backlinks from reputable sites in your niche is important. Tactics like guest blogging, creating shareable infographics, and being active in industry forums can help attract these valuable links. The goal is to build a network of backlinks that boost your site's authority and bring in relevant traffic.

Technical SEO Audits

Regular technical SEO audits are routine check-ups for your site's health. They help identify issues that could affect your site's performance in search engine results, such as slow loading speeds, broken links, or images that need to be optimized. Tools such as Google's Search Console and PageSpeed Insights provide information about your site's performance and areas that need improvement. Fixing these issues immediately ensures that your site stays in good shape and can achieve and maintain high rankings in search engine results.

Implementing These Strategies

Incorporating these advanced SEO techniques requires a balanced approach. Start by revisiting your keyword strategy, ensuring it aligns with current trends and search behaviors. Next, evaluate your site's architecture, making adjustments to improve navigation and crawlability (the ease at which search engine crawlers access your content). Pursue link-building opportunities focusing on quality over quantity and conduct regular technical audits to identify potential issues.

SEO Checklist

An SEO checklist helps you put these advanced SEO methods into practice. Checklist requirements evolve over time; therefore, it is important to check out current examples regularly. The checklist outlines key steps related to keyword research, website structure, link building, and technical audits, providing a step-by-step guide to optimizing your site for search engines. Think of this checklist as your roadmap, ensuring you cover all essential aspects of SEO in your strategy.

In today's fast-paced digital marketing world, mastering advanced SEO techniques is a skill you must master. By emphasizing thorough keyword research, refining website structure, using advanced link-building tactics, and regularly checking technical aspects, you can significantly boost your site's visibility and appeal to search engines and potential customers. This chapter has provided a foundation, offering insights and practical strategies to elevate your SEO efforts. With dedication and smart implementation, navigating the vast digital marketing landscape becomes manageable, leading to increased visibility, engagement, and success in your affiliate marketing ventures.

7.2 PAY-PER-CLICK (PPC) ADVERTISING FOR AFFILIATES: A BEGINNER'S GUIDE

Pay-Per-Click (PPC) advertising stands out as a fundamental tool for affiliates to reach their desired audience directly. With PPC, advertisers pay for each click on their ads, ensuring visits to their website without relying solely on organic traffic. The appeal of PPC for affiliates lies in its precision in driving targeted traffic and flexibility, allowing for careful control over budget, targeting, and ad placements.

Exploring various PPC platforms reveals a range of channels, each offering unique advantages and opportunities. Google Ads, being the giant in this field, provides unmatched visibility across the extensive Google network. Since many online journeys start with a Google search, affiliates have a significant opportunity to highlight their offerings to a motivated audience. Similarly, Bing Ads offers an attractive option with its network covering not just Bing but also Yahoo and AOL. While these platforms may have a smaller share of the search market, they often attract audience segments that are highly engaged and more likely to convert.

A strategic blend of creativity and insight is vital in creating effective ad campaigns on these platforms. Writing audience-grabbing ad copy requires a deep understanding of the product and the audience's needs. The message should be clear yet compelling, emphasizing the unique value of the offering and using key phrases that align with what potential customers are searching for. Choosing relevant keywords is foundational to this process, requiring thorough research to find terms that capture the product's essence and match how the target audience searches. This alignment ensures that ads appear when people search for the product, increasing the chances of engagement.

Effectively handling the PPC budget requires a balanced approach, blending ambition with practicality to get the most out of investments while keeping costs in check. Setting a daily budget sets a spending limit, ensuring expenses stay manageable. However, the real skill lies in dividing this budget among campaigns, keywords, and ad groups, optimizing for performance to focus resources on areas that generate the best returns. This optimization often involves continuous testing and adjustments, refining bids based on performance data to find the right balance between visibility, cost, and conversions.

Analyzing and optimizing campaigns are central to the PPC strategy, where data becomes actionable insights. Using platform analytics tools provides detailed metrics like click-through rates (CTR), conversion rates, and cost per acquisition (CPA), showing how effectively ads engage the target audience and drive desired actions. This analysis includes audience behavior, ad placement effectiveness, and how different keywords and ad variations work together. Insights from this analysis lead to ongoing adjustments, improving underperforming elements and enhancing successful strategies. Additionally, A/B testing, where different ad variations are compared, sharpens this refinement process, helping affiliates fine-tune their PPC strategy for maximum impact.

PPC advertising requires affiliates to navigate platform algorithms, audience behavior, and competition with skill and precision. By mastering PPC platforms, creating ad campaigns that resonate, optimizing budgets for efficiency, and using data for continual improvement, affiliates can use PPC effectively to boost their marketing efforts. This strategic use of PPC enhances visibility, drives targeted traffic, and sets the stage for sustainable growth and success in competitive affiliate marketing.

7.3 CONVERSION RATE OPTIMIZATION: TURNING VISITORS INTO BUYERS

Optimizing landing pages is a top priority for marketers, as they are key places where design, content, and user intent come together to influence a visitor's decision-making process. The goal is to create landing pages that are visually appealing, easy to navigate, and connect with visitors' needs, encouraging them to move from browsing to making a purchase. To achieve this, it's essential to understand what makes successful landing pages work and identify elements that drive conversions. These pages are carefully crafted spaces where every image, headline, and text block is designed to guide visitors toward taking a specific action. Using persuasive, benefit-focused language and relevant images creates a narrative that addresses visitors' needs and desires. At the same time, simplifying design elements and minimizing distractions, such as navigation links, helps keep visitors focused on the conversion goal.

A/B testing is a systematic way to discover the most effective strategies for engaging visitors. Marketers can gather empirical evidence about what works best by testing two-page versions with different elements, such as headlines, images, and calls to action. This continuous testing and refinement based on data provide valuable insights into visitor preferences and behaviors, guiding optimization efforts for better performance aligned with audience preferences.

Enhancing your website's user experience (UX) involves building a captivating path for visitors with simple navigation, quick loading speeds, and a user-friendly design. A positive user experience increases the chances of conversion, so it's essential to identify and address any friction points that may hinder progress or decrease interest. Optimizing page speed to ensure quick content delivery meets users' expectations for immediacy and reduces the risk of them leaving the site. Considering the shift in Internet usage patterns, adapting your site for mobile devices is essential to provide an accessible and enjoyable experience on smaller screens. This comprehensive approach to UX optimization, focusing on both functional and emotional aspects of user interaction, builds a connection with visitors beyond just transactions, leading to higher conversion rates.

Creating effective Calls to Action (CTAs) is crucial for optimizing conversions, as they bridge the gap between visitor interest and taking action. These CTAs represent the pinnacle of a visitor's journey, inviting them clearly and enticingly to proceed. Their success depends on finding the right balance in visibility, persuasiveness, and relevance. They must grab attention without being overwhelmed and placed prominently but seamlessly in the design. The language should be direct yet inviting, showing the value of the action and creating a sense of urgency or exclusivity to encourage engagement. Also, aligning CTAs with the content and context of the page makes them more meaningful to visitors, increasing the chances of conversion. This strategic approach to CTAs, where every detail matters, catalyzes visitors to make decisions, turning their interest into action.

Optimizing conversion strategies demonstrates a marketer's dedication to attracting and engaging visitors effectively. By focusing on refining landing pages, using A/B testing strategically, improving user experience, and creating compelling CTAs, marketers navigate consumer behavior intricacies with precision. This method, grounded in understanding visitors' needs and backed by real data, goes beyond surface-level tactics, diving into the psychology of conversion. Here, at the intersection of strategy, design, and content, lies the potential to turn visitors into customers, marking not the end but a milestone in the ongoing journey of optimization and growth.

7.4 ANALYZING AND ADJUSTING YOUR TRAFFIC STRATEGIES

Successfully drawing, understanding, and reacting to the flow of visitors to your affiliate marketing projects requires strategic thinking and flexibility. Effectively monitoring how traffic is generated is a valuable strategy in shaping the paths that guide visitors to your online presence. Balancing attraction and analysis at this intersection is where traffic strategies gain power, requiring attention to the big picture and the finer details of traffic movements.

Integrating key performance metrics into traffic analysis is central to this effort. Metrics including sessions, page views, bounce rate, and average session duration give a broad view of traffic activity, showing how visitors interact with your online platform. However, the real value of these metrics lies in their ability to uncover the nuances of visitor engagement, going beyond numbers to reveal meaningful interactions. So, refining traffic strategies starts with carefully evaluating these metrics and identifying patterns, highlighting strengths and areas needing improvement.

The next phase involves diving deeper into the story behind the numbers. Tools that track visitors' paths through your site and analytics that break down traffic sources provide a comprehensive understanding of how different strategies impact overall traffic. This detailed analysis, enriched by insights into your audience's demographics and behavior, guides the ongoing optimization process. It helps make adjustments that better align with visitor preferences and behaviors, aiming not just to react but to anticipate trends using data as a guide.

Within this framework, repetitive optimization becomes a continuous journey of improvement based on real evidence. It involves constantly refining strategies by tweaking content, adjusting keywords, and fine-tuning promotional efforts to better resonate with your target audience. Being agile in responding to data-driven insights ensures traffic strategies remain adaptable and aligned with evolving audience preferences. The iterative process embodies the principle that in digital marketing, staying stagnant is counterproductive to achieving success.

However, there are moments along this path when making small changes isn't enough, indicating the necessity to change how traffic is generated. These pivotal decisions are based on a combination of data, market trends, and a deep understanding of how the audience behaves. Deciding to pivot may come from shifts in the online world, changes in how consumers act, or the introduction of new platforms and technologies. Knowing when and how to pivot depends on the ability to distinguish between temporary changes and fundamental shifts, requiring a strategic approach grounded in data and awareness of the broader trends in digital marketing. Making a pivot isn't a sign of failure but a strategic move, recognizing that success often involves exploring new directions.

By bringing together performance metrics, data analysis, continuous improvement, and strategic pivots, the story of traffic strategies becomes a complex yet promising journey. This chapter has explored the world of traffic generation, focusing on how strategy and analysis interact, stressing the importance of using data to navigate digital marketing. Progress in this area requires ongoing learning, adjusting, and strategically realigning efforts to connect more deeply with the target audience. As we move from discussing traffic strategies to broader topics in affiliate marketing, the knowledge gained here becomes a strong foundation and guiding principle for achieving excellence in digital marketing. The road ahead is full of challenges and opportunities, inviting us to continue with curiosity, resilience, and strategic planning for success.

AMPLIFYING YOUR AFFILIATE MARKETING THROUGH SOCIAL MEDIA

Picture a vibrant market where everything from conversations to transactions unfolds instantly. That's the heart of social media—a lively, always-changing space where brands and customers meet, stories develop, and buying choices are shaped. The power of social media in boosting your affiliate marketing is like discovering rich soil where content seeds can be planted, cared for, and eventually reaped for significant benefits.

8.1 SOCIAL MEDIA STRATEGIES FOR AMPLIFYING YOUR REACH

Platform Selection

Selecting the right social media platforms is like choosing a venue for an event. It depends on knowing where your audience hangs out online, how they use social media, and what interactions they prefer. For example, Instagram, focusing on visuals, is great for lifestyle products, while LinkedIn is better suited for B2B services.

Each platform has unique traits and audiences, so picking one that matches your affiliate marketing goals and your audience's preferences is crucial.

Content Strategy for Social Media

Crafting a social media content strategy goes beyond sharing links. It's about creating content that resonates, grabs attention, and adds value to your audience's online experience. Use each platform's special features—like Instagram stories or Twitter polls—to authenticate your followers. Mix your content with educational posts, reviews, and personal stories about your affiliate products. This approach makes your promotions feel natural and integrated into your social media presence.

Paid Social Advertising

Paid social advertising can boost your affiliate marketing efforts by expanding your reach. Platforms like Facebook and Instagram let you target specific demographics, interests, and behaviors, ensuring your ads reach the right people. To make the most of paid ads, craft compelling copy and visuals, test different elements to see what works best, and adjust your targeting based on your campaigns' performance.

Measuring Social Media Success

Measuring social media success involves looking at metrics like engagement, click-through rates, and conversions. Platforms offer tools to see how your content and ads are doing and who's interacting with them. For affiliates, tracking conversions from social media to actual sales is vital, which means tracking links and monitoring tools to link sales to specific social media activities.

This data shows how well your current efforts work and helps shape future strategies by refining targeting, content, and promotional tactics for better outcomes.

Social Media Performance Dashboard

Many platforms offer an interactive dashboard to help marketers track and analyze social media efforts. The dashboard tool consolidates important metrics from social media platforms, giving a full picture of campaign performance, audience engagement, and conversions. The dashboard can be customized based on specific goals and metrics, providing a real-time view of social media success and areas that need improvement.

Using social media for affiliate marketing requires a smart, adaptable approach to the digital world's changes. Choosing the right platforms, creating engaging content, using paid ads, and measuring success are all critical parts of a strategy that boosts visibility and maximizes the impact of affiliate marketing efforts. With careful planning and ongoing improvements, social media becomes a promotional tool and a lively community where connections are made, trust is built, and affiliate marketing goals are met.

8.2 THE POWER OF INFLUENCER MARKETING IN AFFILIATE STRATEGIES

Collaborating with influencers stands out as a unique opportunity with promise and challenges. This collaboration goes beyond just promoting products; it taps into the trust and connection influencers have built with their followers. Finding and teaming up with these online personalities requires a careful approach that looks beyond just matching audience demographics – it involves aligning values, authenticity, and a natural fit for your affiliate offerings.

The first step in building these partnerships is curating a guest list for an exclusive event. The goal is to ensure that each influencer's style, audience interaction, and content align with your brand's identity and marketing goals. There are tools available that provide data on an influencer's reach, engagement rates, and content quality. Equally important is understanding the qualitative aspects of an influencer's impact – how they talk about products, the genuine connections they create, and their ability to influence purchases without being pushy.

Once potential influencers are identified, the focus shifts to planning campaigns in a flexible but adaptable way. The goals of these campaigns can vary from increasing brand visibility and directing traffic to specific pages to engaging with your content or boosting sales. The campaign plan must outline the desired outcomes and details like content types, posting schedules, and tracking methods to monitor performance. Collaborating closely with influencers during this planning phase ensures a shared vision and a coordinated approach, setting the stage for campaigns that resonate and achieve their goals.

Negotiating and establishing contracts with influencers involves finding a balance between giving them creative freedom while ensuring they align with the goals of your campaign. While this process is often seen as business-like, it's important for building a partnership based on mutual understanding and shared objectives. These discussions should openly cover expectations, what each party will deliver, payment details, and any legal requirements, ensuring that both sides know how the collaboration will work. Negotiations lead to formal contracts outlining these agreements, creating a structured framework that protects your interests and the influencers. These agreements solidify the partnership, showing the collaborative spirit behind the campaign.

Monitoring and utilizing influencer content during the campaign goes beyond just watching – it's about actively engaging to maximize the content's impact. This requires monitoring metrics such as engagement rates, clicks, and conversions and finding ways to share this content widely across your platforms. The shared content becomes a powerful tool that reinforces the campaign's messages, reaches a larger audience, and adds credibility. Tools that gather data from different platforms provide valuable insights, allowing you to adjust your campaign strategies in real-time based on how your audience responds. This monitoring phase turns the campaign into a dynamic entity that evolves and improves through active engagement and smart adjustments.

Integrating influencer marketing strategically into your affiliate strategies can open new opportunities for connecting with your audience and growing your brand. The careful process of working with influencers, from finding the right ones to monitoring the campaign, requires planning and a commitment to building authentic partnerships. These collaborations, based on shared values and goals, go beyond traditional marketing, offering a way to connect with audiences genuinely and trustworthy. Navigating this intersection of influence, content, and strategy can significantly enhance your affiliate marketing efforts, creating connections that truly engage and drive conversions.

8.3 EMAIL LIST BUILDING: STRATEGIES FOR LONG-TERM SUCCESS

An email list isn't just a list of contacts; it's more like a carefully tended garden. Each subscriber is like a seed that has the potential to grow and bring results. This garden thrives on careful nurturing, where building relationships through personalized communication is key for long-term success. The core of this effort involves creating attractive lead magnets, using different strategies to get people to sign up, setting up automated emails, and using segmentation and personalization effectively. These elements work together to create a strong email list plan.

Lead Magnets

Lead magnets are the bait that attracts visitors to your list. Creating a successful lead magnet requires a good understanding of your audience's wants and struggles. You convert this knowledge into an irresistible offer encouraging visitors to give you their contact details. Lead magnets can take many forms, including eBooks packed with niche knowledge, templates that simplify complex tasks, exclusive webinars with industry experts, or tools designed to solve specific problems. Crafting these magnets requires creativity and careful consideration of their value, ensuring they match your audience's expectations and needs.

Opt-in Strategies

After setting up your lead magnet to attract interest, the focus turns to opt-in strategies to convert visitors into subscribers. During this phase, a wide range of tactics, from subtle to more direct approaches, are carefully designed to blend seamlessly into the user experience without causing disruptions. For example, when timed right, pop-ups can grab attention when visitors are most engaged, presenting the lead magnet as a natural addition to the content they're already consuming. Landing pages, which are dedicated pages focused solely on highlighting the value of the lead magnet, act as a clear pathway, guiding visitors to subscribe with compelling calls to action. Content upgrades offer extra value within existing content, appealing to highly engaged visitors and giving them an immediate reason to subscribe. Using this strategic mix of opt-in methods, we ensure a smooth transition from casual visitor to engaged subscriber, enriching our metaphorical garden with each new addition.

Email Automation

Email automation is an advanced tool that delivers targeted and timely communication to subscribers. Automation platforms act like the watering systems for our garden, ensuring each plant gets just the right amount of water at the perfect time—no more and no less. This technology allows us to create drip campaigns that gently guide subscribers through a sequence of emails, each one building on the last to encourage engagement and move toward conversion. Welcome sequences introduce new subscribers to your brand, while specific actions can trigger follow-up sequences, like downloading a lead magnet or leaving a shopping cart. This automated approach ensures that each subscriber's interactions with your content are acknowledged and responded to in a way that feels personal, even though it's happening on a larger scale.

Segmentation and Personalization

The final and most important step is segmentation and personalization, which are practices that recognize each subscriber's unique characteristics and interests and customize communication accordingly. Segmentation involves organizing your email list based on factors like age, how engaged subscribers are, what they've bought before, and what they've shown interest in. This divides your list into different groups with traits and preferences. Personalization takes this further by using data from segmentation to create emails that directly speak to each person, addressing them by name, mentioning their specific interests, and suggesting things that align with their past interactions with your brand. This level of personalization goes beyond generic emails, creating a sense of connection and relevance that improves the subscriber's experience, leading to more engagement and conversions.

Overall, the strategies discussed here form a complete approach to building an email list that recognizes the complexity and diversity of subscriber relationships. Each part is instrumental in growing and nurturing your email list, from attracting subscribers with lead magnets to using segmentation and personalization for tailored communication. This approach, characterized by careful planning and a focus on providing value and relevance, sets the groundwork for success in affiliate marketing, transforming your list of subscribers into an active community that engages and converts effectively.

8.4 LEVERAGING FORUMS AND ONLINE COMMUNITIES

Forums and online communities offer great opportunities for building genuine connections. These spaces allow people to share ideas, solve problems, and exchange experiences, creating a strong sense of belonging. For affiliate marketers, engaging in these communities requires a thoughtful approach focused on providing value and showing respect in every interaction. Discovering active communities involves careful observation and understanding of where your target audience gathers online. Platforms like Reddit, with its diverse subreddits covering various interests and specialized forums focusing on specific topics, offer numerous opportunities for those willing to invest time in learning about their unique cultures and communication styles.

Finding the right communities involves immersing yourself in their discussions, appreciating their values, and understanding how people interact there. While tools and analytics can give you insights into demographics and engagement levels, truly grasping a community's essence comes from actively participating in conversations. Engaging with these communities starts with listening and observing to grasp the main themes, the tone of discussions, and the content that resonates most with members.

When engaging in forums and online communities, balancing contributing value and promoting your affiliate offers is key. Initial interactions should focus on providing helpful comments, insightful advice, and sharing knowledge without pushing your promotions. This approach builds trust and credibility, showing you're a valuable member who enriches the community. Once trust is established, subtly promoting your content and affiliate offers will become more acceptable. Sharing content that addresses community needs or answers questions while being transparent about your affiliate relationships is better received when it's clear that your main goal is to help rather than solely to make a profit.

Sharing and promoting content in forums and online communities should be done tactfully, considering the context and ongoing conversations. Content that adds value to discussions or provides solutions is appreciated, while content that seems out of place or forced might face resistance. Knowing when and how to share content requires being dedicated to the community and participating in discussions without expecting immediate benefits. Using affiliate links and promotional content sparingly is important, preferably alongside informative content or responding to queries where your affiliate products can genuinely help.

Successful engagement in forums and online communities revolves around building real relationships. This goes beyond just transactional interactions; it's about creating connections based on shared interests, mutual respect, and a sincere desire to contribute. Building relationships in these spaces takes time and requires patience and authenticity. Being actively involved in discussions, offering assistance without expecting anything, and showing genuine interest in others' opinions and experiences helps establish you as a valued community member. Over time, these relationships can lead to organic promotion, as community members who trust and respect you are more likely to engage with your content, consider your recommendations, and support your affiliate marketing efforts.

Utilizing forums and online communities for affiliate marketing is about connecting with people authentically. It involves a strategic approach that prioritizes providing value, showing respect, and being genuine. Affiliate marketers engage with these digital spaces to honor their culture and enhance their discussions. By engaging thoughtfully, promoting subtly, and dedicating themselves to building authentic relationships, affiliate marketers can unlock the vast potential of these platforms, using engagement as a powerful tool for growth and connection.

8.5 CREATIVE CONTENT DISTRIBUTION TACTICS

Creating content is just one part of reaching and engaging an audience. The challenge and the chance to succeed come from sharing this content across different platforms, connecting each with its audience and expectations. You need a strategic plan to ensure your created content reaches the right people and has a big impact.

Syndication

Syndication is a key tool in this strategy. It lets you share your content on other websites with established audiences, reaching new parts of your target audience that you might only go to if you reach them. Syndication helps with SEO by getting more backlinks and bringing direct traffic to your site. However, you must be careful when choosing where to syndicate your content. Pick sites that match your content's quality, style, and topic to benefit both sides. It's also important to negotiate terms that respect your rights to your content while making the most of syndication's reach.

Guest Posting

Guest posting is another smart way to get your content out there. You can reach new audiences and build credibility in your niche by writing guest posts for respected blogs and digital publications. To get these opportunities, you need to know the content landscape well and find platforms that share an audience with you. When pitching guest post ideas, focus on offering value to the host site's audience and filling gaps in their content. Successful guest posts bring traffic to your site through links and boost your reputation in your niche, showing that your insights are valuable and respected.

Collaborations

Collaborating with other content creators opens new avenues for distributing content beyond syndication and guest posting. These partnerships, which can involve co-authored pieces, joint webinars, or podcast episodes, bring together different perspectives and audiences, exposing your content to fresh segments of your target market.

Successful collaborations rely on finding partners whose content style and audience align with yours, ensuring the partnership delivers value to both sides. The process of co-creating content enhances its quality and builds a sense of community among creators and their audiences, expanding the reach and impact of the shared content.

Repurposing Content

Another effective strategy is repurposing content, which taps into the idea that creativity knows no bounds. This approach involves transforming existing content into different formats tailored to various audience preferences. For example, a detailed blog post can be turned into an infographic, a series of social media posts, or a video tutorial. Repurposing content extends its reach and caters to diverse audience tastes, maximizing the return on your content creation efforts. The key to successful repurposing lies in choosing formats that complement your original content and connect with your audience, ensuring that each repurposed piece adds value while contributing to your brand's overall message.

A strategic approach that includes syndication, guest posting, collaborations, and content repurposing is essential to navigate the complex content distribution landscape. This strategy must be adaptable and creative, responding to audience preferences and digital platform changes. By carefully selecting distribution channels, forming partnerships, and creatively repurposing content, you can turn content distribution into a strategic advantage rather than just a logistical challenge.

8.6 RETARGETING: CAPTURING LOST OPPORTUNITIES

Retargeting brings back people who visited your site but have yet to make a purchase or take action. It's about reigniting their interest and guiding them back to complete what they started, whether buying or signing up for something. This technique uses cookies or pixel tags, small bits of code on your website that quietly track visitors. These tools help create ads that remind people of their interests.

Platforms like Google Ads and Facebook Ads are crucial for running these retargeting campaigns. They provide tools to put your ads in front of potential customers, regardless of where they are online. Setting up these campaigns requires understanding your audience's behavior, creating engaging ads, and using your budget wisely.

Segmentation plays a big role in making retargeting effective. It involves sorting your audience based on how they behave on your site or their interests. This way, you can tailor ads to specific groups, making them more likely to convert. For example, someone who left items in their cart might be tempted back with a special deal, while someone who read product reviews could see ads highlighting those products' benefits. The better you segment your audience, the more personalized and effective your retargeting efforts become, turning generic ads into personalized messages that acknowledge each visitor's unique journey.

Measuring the success of retargeting goes beyond just counting clicks and views. It focuses on more meaningful metrics like conversion rates, cost per conversion, and return on ad spend (ROAS). These metrics clearly show how well your retargeting efforts work financially, allowing you to improve constantly. A/B testing, where you compare different ad elements, is valuable in finding what works best. Also, combining retargeting data with broader marketing analytics gives a full view of how ads impact customer journeys and overall brand engagement.

Using retargeting in affiliate marketing recognizes that customer journeys are sometimes complicated. It sees potential in initial interactions that might not lead to immediate conversions but can be revived later. This approach shows sophistication in tactics and respect for engaging audiences, adapting to the ever-changing digital marketing landscape where seemingly lost opportunities can succeed.

In the vast array of digital marketing strategies, retargeting brings people back based on understanding what works with how consumers behave. Through careful segmentation, setting up targeted campaigns, and rigorous tracking, lost chances are reclaimed, guiding visitors back to finish what they started. This discussion on retargeting emphasizes its role in building meaningful connections with your audience, providing valuable insights for navigating advanced techniques and new trends in digital marketing.

MAXIMIZING EARNINGS: ADVANCED AFFILIATE MONETIZATION STRATEGIES

Affiliate marketers face both opportunities and challenges in a rapidly changing digital world. With the internet's vast reach, anyone can share their voice, making it vital to have strategies that go beyond the usual to capture and keep an audience's attention. This section explores advanced methods for earning more and building a strong foundation in affiliate marketing.

9.1 STRATEGIC PRODUCT SELECTION

Choosing which products to promote requires an understanding of how to make money as an affiliate. High-value products can bring in big commissions with each sale, while those with recurring commissions offer a steady income that adds up over time. It's like investing in stocks, balancing riskier but potentially rewarding choices with stable, long-term investments to create a diverse portfolio.

Product Selection Flowchart

A flowchart can help you select affiliate products. It considers commission rates, how relevant a product is to your audience, market demand, and how long customers keep buying. This makes the process easier, guiding you toward smart choices that match your financial goals and your audience's wants.

Leveraging Data for Upselling

Data analytics can help you spot opportunities to upsell, where you introduce additional products or premium versions based on your audience's buying habits and interactions. Convincing a customer to purchase an extended warranty for a product they purchased is an example of upselling. This increases how much each customer spends and improves their experience by offering suggestions that match their changing preferences and needs.

Cross-platform Promotion

Promoting products across different platforms is a key strategy, as each platform has unique strengths and audiences. This cross-platform approach can range from visually appealing Instagram posts to engaging Twitter discussions and personalized emails. Combining different elements to create a story that connects with people wherever they are most active is the undercurrent of this strategy.

Platform Optimization Checklist

A platform optimization checklist can help tailor your promotions for each platform, ensuring your content is engaging and effective. It covers everything from using the right hashtags and images to crafting compelling email subject lines and webinar formats, giving you a roadmap for successful cross-platform promotion. Platform optimization requirements evolve quickly in a dynamic technological world. Research different examples of optimization checklists for the key platforms you choose.

Membership and Subscription Models

Membership and subscription models offer a steady income stream. Incorporating these models into your strategy involves finding products or services that continuously benefit consumers, ensuring that your offer meets their needs. This alignment, like subscribing to a magazine that consistently delivers value, turns one-time buyers into long-term subscribers, boosting their value to your affiliate efforts and creating a stable financial base.

Advanced strategies in affiliate marketing require innovation, foresight, and a deep understanding of the digital market. By choosing products strategically, using data to upsell, promoting across multiple platforms, and incorporating membership/subscriptions, marketers can unlock higher earnings and build a sustainable path to success. While these strategies require effort, they hold the potential to reshape affiliate marketing, offering a guide for those ready to explore beyond the basics.

9.2 SCALING YOUR AFFILIATE MARKETING EFFORTS: WHEN AND HOW

Expanding your affiliate marketing is necessary for steady growth and profits. Scaling up involves analyzing your current efforts carefully, investing strategically in content creation, exploring new areas, and building crucial relationships for expansion. You must consider trends and what customers want now.

To scale effectively, you must examine your current affiliate activities. This requires looking at performance data to find products or campaigns that bring the most returns and have room to grow—metrics like conversion rates and customer value show where you can profit. Engagement stats including clicks and social media interactions help focus efforts on areas with the most growth potential.

Putting profits back into creating top-notch content is key to growing your affiliate marketing. Valuable content attracts and keeps an audience, setting the stage for successful affiliate promotions. This goes beyond typical blog posts, including videos, webinars, interactive tools, and more. Each content, well-crafted and strategically shared, pulls in potential customers. This content-focused approach also boosts your brand's reputation, leading to more conversions and funds for creating even better content.

Diversifying income sources and reducing market risks involves carefully entering new niches rather than just jumping in. You must thoroughly study these areas to ensure they match your strengths and your audience's wants. Market research tools and keyword analysis help find profitable niches by showing gaps in the market. Understanding the new niche's audience—their needs, likes, and problems—is crucial to ensure your offer is valuable and fits in well. Branching out into related niches expands your reach and makes your business more stable against market changes.

Building strategic partnerships and connecting with industry peers opens doors to opportunities you might need help to reach. These relationships, built on ongoing engagement and mutual support, can lead to exclusive affiliate programs, joint marketing efforts, and insights into new trends. Being active in industry events, online communities, and social media helps you connect with influencers and learn from experts. Collaborating with other affiliates or content creators can lead to projects that benefit everyone involved, increasing your reach and credibility through shared expertise.

Scaling up affiliate marketing involves smart resource allocation, exploring new areas, and building strong relationships within the industry. This journey focuses on steady growth and staying relevant in the ever-changing digital marketing world.

9.3 DIVERSIFYING YOUR AFFILIATE INCOME: A STRATEGY FOR STABILITY

Change is constant and unpredictable in the digital marketplace, shaping the world where affiliate marketers seek success. Diversification leads toward a future where stability and growth come together. Affiliate marketing diversifying involves a range of strategies to strengthen financial security against market shifts.

Multiple Affiliate Programs

Working with multiple affiliate programs is like spreading investments across stocks to reduce risk. Relying on just one program can be risky due to commission changes, product popularity, or program closure. Selecting these programs requires careful consideration to find ones that match your audience's interests and offer mutually beneficial terms. By vetting potential programs based on their history, product quality, and support, you ensure they align with your brand's values and long-term goals. This diversity of programs adds resilience and vitality to your affiliate efforts.

Combining Affiliate Marketing with Other Revenue Streams

Moving beyond traditional affiliate marketing means exploring other income sources. This evolution can involve creating and selling digital products like eBooks or courses tailored to your audience's needs. Offering consulting services or coaching in your niche is another way to generate income while building stronger connections with your audience. Membership sites provide exclusive content and community interactions for a recurring fee and create consistent revenue streams. These ventures diversify income and enhance your brand's appeal, fostering loyalty and adding value for your audience.

Investing in Paid Traffic

While organic reach is cost-effective, it can take much work, especially during early site growth or new campaign launches. Paid traffic campaigns, like those on Google Ads or Facebook Ads, can accelerate visibility and engagement. These platforms allow precise targeting to reach specific audience segments accurately. However, investing in paid traffic requires careful planning and monitoring to optimize performance. By diversifying customer acquisition avenues, paid traffic reduces reliance on search engine algorithms and social media trends. When executed well, paid traffic boosts reach and speeds up growth, adding flexibility and responsiveness to your affiliate marketing strategy.

Geographic Expansion

The online world, limitless in its scope, brings together people worldwide seeking solutions, entertainment, and connections. When affiliate marketing expands to cover different regions or countries, it's not just about reaching more people but smartly spreading risk across markets. This expansion requires a deep understanding of cultural differences, consumers' behavior, and preferred languages. It means tailoring content, promotions, and products to fit each new audience. Market research tools help identify promising new markets and guide strategies to suit local needs. Partnering with local influencers or brands can also help break into these markets by lending credibility and tapping into existing trust. By expanding geographically, affiliate marketers reach a wider audience with diverse needs, creating a safety net against market difficulties.

Diversification is key to stability and growth in the vast field of affiliate marketing. Affiliate marketers build a strong foundation that can withstand digital market shifts by joining multiple affiliate programs, integrating various income streams, investing strategically in paid advertising, and venturing into new global markets. This strategic approach, focusing on planning and adapting, protects against risks from individual income sources and fosters a vibrant, varied ecosystem where success continues despite changes.

9.4 BUILDING AND MANAGING AFFILIATE PARTNERSHIPS

Choosing and nurturing partnerships is crucial for long-term success. Selecting affiliate partners involves finding products that align with the audience's interests and values, forming a strong foundation for collaboration. First, it's important to dive deep into the audience's preferences using data from various sources including social media, emails, and website analytics. This helps paint a clear picture of what the audience wants and needs, making it easier to find partners whose offerings match these profiles, leading to a seamless integration of products into your content.

Negotiating partnership terms requires diplomacy and a focus on mutual benefit. You need to showcase what you bring to the table, such as access to a specific audience, expertise in creating content, or strong marketing skills. At the same time, it's crucial to outline your expectations regarding commissions, promotional support, and product access. The goal is to create an agreement that benefits both parties and fosters a sense of fairness and shared success. This negotiation phase lays the groundwork for a relationship of transparency, respect, and common goals.

Maintaining these relationships over time involves ongoing communication and collaboration. Regular check-ins, updates, and meetings facilitate an exchange of ideas, feedback, and strategies that can adapt to market changes. This proactive engagement strengthens the partnership and fosters a sense of teamwork and mutual support, which are essential for navigating the digital marketplace's challenges. Additionally, recognizing and celebrating achievements, like successful campaigns or partnership anniversaries, helps create a culture of appreciation and acknowledgment, further solidifying the bond between affiliates and partners.

Leveraging partnerships for mutual growth embodies synergy, where collaboration surpasses individual efforts. Co-marketing ventures like joint webinars or cross-promotions reach broader audiences, combining strengths for greater impact. Exclusive offers, such as special discounts or unique bundles, boost sales and loyalty. Based on understanding partners' strengths and audiences, this strategic approach drives innovation and prosperity in affiliate marketing.

Building and managing affiliate partnerships requires strategic planning and genuine engagement. From selecting partners aligned with audience values to fostering dynamic relationships and leveraging collaborations, each step contributes to affiliate marketing success. Transparency, respect, and shared goals guide this journey, ensuring partnerships achieve their aims and enhance affiliate endeavors.

Exploring advanced strategies for maximizing earnings and fostering sustainable partnerships highlights their interconnectedness. Careful product selection, data-driven upselling, expansion across platforms and regions, and nurturing partnerships create a holistic affiliate marketing approach. This chapter prepares us to adapt, innovate, and lead in the dynamic affiliate marketing landscape ahead.

NAVIGATING TOMORROW'S TERRAIN: THE FUTURE OF AFFILIATE MARKETING

Affiliate marketing is a predictor of how the digital economy will evolve. This field is shaped by innovation, with each new idea pushing boundaries and exploring new territories where change is the only sure thing. This chapter delves into these possibilities, looking at how emerging technologies and changing behaviors are set to transform affiliate marketing.

10.1 CHANGES IN THE AFFILIATE MARKETING LANDSCAPE

Emerging Technologies: AI and Machine Learning

Picture yourself on the shore of a vast ocean filled with unknown creatures, each wave hiding mysteries from the depths. That ocean is where affiliate marketing is headed, with technologies like AI and machine learning opening uncharted territories. These tools, once the stuff of sci-fi, are now part of everyday life, offering exciting chances for personalization and efficiency in affiliate marketing.

AI's ability to analyze data turns heaps of information into practical insights, accurately predicting how consumers will behave. Machine learning algorithms improve these predictions over time, getting smarter with each interaction and making affiliate offers more relevant. These technologies predict and automate tasks like sorting emails and creating content, giving marketers more time to focus on strategy and creativity.

Changing Consumer Behaviors

The digital era has triggered significant changes in consumers' expectations, emphasizing immediacy, convenience, and personalized experiences. This shift in consumer behavior requires a corresponding evolution in affiliate marketing strategies. For example, the growing popularity of voice search calls for optimizing content to suit conversational queries. At the same time, the desire for personalization necessitates using data to customize offers based on individual preferences.

Adapting to these changes involves seeing consumers not as targets but as active participants in an ongoing conversation. This change places high value on authenticity and meaningful engagement, transforming every interaction point, whether on social media or through email, into a chance for genuine connection.

Consumer Behavior Timeline

Research historical consumer behavior timelines for the specific products and services you plan to offer through your affiliate marketing business. A comprehensive timeline maps out key changes in consumer behavior over the last decade. It highlights milestones like the surge in mobile commerce, the emergence of voice search, and the increased demand for sustainable products. This visual tool puts these shifts into context, showing how they impact affiliate marketing strategies.

Regulatory and Privacy Changes

Amidst technological progress, there's a growing focus on regulatory adjustments, emphasizing the ethical responsibilities that come with digital marketing power. Implementing regulations such as GDPR in Europe and CCPA in California marks a significant shift in data protection standards, requiring marketers to prioritize transparency and user consent in data handling.

Responding to these changes requires a proactive approach, integrating privacy considerations into the core of affiliate marketing campaigns. This adaptation goes beyond mere compliance, recognizing privacy as essential for building trust between marketers and consumers. The future of affiliate marketing in this regulated environment hinges on finding a balance between personalization and privacy, a delicate act that requires both technological expertise and ethical dedication.

Compliance Checklist

Research data privacy regulations for the regions you plan to include in your target audience. Create a checklist of regulatory considerations for each area. Regulatory laws for technology change quickly, based on new technology challenges faced. Update this checklist regularly to ensure you address significant changes in rules and regulations proactively. A detailed checklist provides essential steps for ensuring adherence to data privacy regulations. It covers everything from implementing consent mechanisms to establishing robust data protection measures. This tool is a roadmap for affiliate marketers navigating the intricate regulatory environment.

Innovations in Affiliate Marketing

Innovations stand out like guiding lights in the future of affiliate marketing, signaling pathways to continued growth. Take blockchain technology, for example, offering transparency and security in affiliate transactions by reducing fraud and enhancing trust. Similarly, augmented reality (AR) brings immersive experiences that transform how products are discovered and promoted, making passive viewing interactive.

Though still emerging, these innovations represent the forefront of affiliate marketing's evolution. They challenge marketers to think beyond current boundaries, viewing these technologies not as distant dreams but as imminent realities. Embracing these changes positions affiliate marketers as pioneers in the industry's evolution, ready to navigate the unknown territories of tomorrow's digital landscape.

Case Study: Blockchain in Affiliate Marketing

A detailed examination delves into how blockchain technology is used in an affiliate marketing campaign, focusing on its impact on transparency, commission tracking, and fraud reduction. This real-world example provides valuable insights into how blockchain can change affiliate marketing and shows its potential to reshape the entire industry.

The convergence of new technologies, changing consumer behaviors, regulatory shifts, and innovations presents challenges and opportunities for the future of affiliate marketing. This chapter acts as a guide, helping marketers navigate the complexities of the digital world. The future holds the promise of change, and it invites affiliate marketers to anticipate and influence that change, creating a path toward growth, creativity, and lasting success in the dynamic realm of digital commerce.

10.2 ADVANCED SEO TECHNIQUES FOR AFFILIATE MARKETERS

In the expansive realm of digital marketing, there's a noticeable shift towards more advanced SEO strategies, which shed light on techniques previously hidden by complex algorithms. This section uncovers these sophisticated SEO methods, which aim to boost the visibility of affiliate marketing efforts and enhance the user experience. The goal is to create a digital environment where being relevant and accessible is key.

In-depth Keyword Research

The core of effective SEO lies in digging deeper into keyword research. This process goes beyond surface-level terms to uncover long-tail and intent-based phrases a thoughtful audience is searching. It's a thorough process that uses tools to analyze search patterns, revealing what potential visitors are specifically looking for. Focusing on long-tail keywords, which are specific and have less competition, gives a strategic edge by aligning content with the precise needs of an audience ready to convert. Intent-based keywords take this further, categorizing searches into informational, navigational, and transactional, each needing a tailored content strategy to meet searchers' implicit desires and expectations. Though this deep dive into keyword research requires effort, it connects content and what searchers want. It creates an environment where being relevant is crucial, and engagement is likely.

Site Speed Optimization

Online, quick site loading is required, as users value fast experiences. Optimizing site speed is a critical task that combines technical skills and strategic planning. Speed-up techniques range from compressing images and using browser caching to streamlining CSS, JavaScript, and HTML files to reduce load times and enhance user experience. Content delivery networks (CDNs) take this further by spreading content across multiple servers, reducing delays, and ensuring fast access regardless of location. This emphasis on speed improves user experience and pleases search engines, as speed is a major factor in their ranking algorithms. This dual focus on user satisfaction and search visibility creates a seamless story of efficiency and accessibility.

Structured Data Implementation

Implementing structured data helps search engines understand and present information better, increasing visibility and click-through rates. By using schemas to markup content, web pages can accurately distinguish different elements like reviews, products, and articles. This clarity improves how content appears in search results with features like snippets and knowledge graphs, effectively matching content with search intent. This strategic use of structured data optimized content and tells compelling stories that invite engagement and exploration.

Backlink Acquisition Strategies

In SEO, backlinks are connections that tie the online world together, showing relevance and authority. Getting high-quality backlinks from trusted sources shows your content is valuable and credible. However, affiliate marketers must focus on backlinks of high quality and relevance. Creating content that naturally attracts links because of its insights or unique perspective is one strategy. Personalized outreach to respected sites, suggesting collaborations, or sharing valuable content is another. Guest blogging on reputable platforms can also help gain backlinks when done thoughtfully. Building backlinks with integrity and strategy boosts your site's authority and creates a network of connections that guide visitors through the digital landscape.

In advanced SEO, affiliate marketers must adapt to changing search engine algorithms and anticipate shifts in digital behavior. This requires continuous learning, embracing complexity, and building meaningful connections beyond just transactions. Advanced SEO techniques show the way to a future where content and searchers interact seamlessly in a journey of discovery and satisfaction.

10.3 AUTOMATION AND TOOLS FOR SCALING YOUR BUSINESS

Automation tools are digital helpers that are advanced yet user-friendly, freeing marketers from repetitive tasks so they can focus on growth and innovation. They handle tasks like managing email campaigns that reach potential leads directly and scheduling content for consistent engagement across platforms, boosting productivity.

Automating social media management involves analyzing engagement patterns to adjust real-time strategies for online communities. These tools use algorithms to predict the best times to post and the most popular audience content, expanding a marketer's reach online. Email marketing tools segment audiences precisely, crafting personalized messages that build loyalty and drive conversions.

In parallel, Customer Relationship Management (CRM) systems provide a comprehensive view of customer interactions, capturing every detail from first contact to conversion. These systems track and analyze data to help build lasting relationships. By offering a unified view of customer information, CRM systems empower marketers to anticipate needs, personalize communications, and deliver top-notch service, making the customer journey seamless and satisfying.

Advanced analytics and tracking tools add depth to this marketplace, providing clear insights into data patterns that inform decision-making. These tools chart campaign performance, highlighting peaks of engagement and valleys of disinterest. By combining data from various sources, analytics tools create a cohesive view of marketing effectiveness, shifting from gut instincts to evidence-based decisions.

However, improving growth and efficiency demands recognition of tasks beyond automation or requiring specialized knowledge leads to strategic outsourcing and delegation. This shift, identifying time-consuming or complex tasks and assigning them to external experts or dedicated team members, reflects a mature business strategy. By delegating content creation, technical SEO, or graphic design, marketers optimize resources and bring diverse expertise to their campaigns, adding creativity and innovation to their marketing strategies.

In orchestrating operational elements, from automation tools managing marketing efforts to CRM systems capturing customer relationships and analytics revealing campaign performance, efficiency emerges. This efficiency, supported by strategic task allocation through outsourcing and delegation, propels marketers into productive and strategic realms previously obscured. In this liberated environment, time becomes an asset and insights a guide, fostering growth and innovation in affiliate marketing through excellence and strategic technology use.

10.4 CRAFTING HIGH-CONVERTING AFFILIATE LANDING PAGES

Crafting an affiliate landing page is akin to staging a theatrical performance, where each aspect, from visual to text, plays a vital role in engaging the audience. This part explores the strategies derived from marketing psychology, design aesthetics, and analytical precision to turn passive viewers into active participants in the affiliated store.

Landing Page Design Principles

The first impression of a landing page, like the opening act of a play, shapes how visitors perceive the experience, making design principles guidelines and the foundation of effective communication. Simplicity reduces distractions, focusing visitors on the main message and the call to action (CTA). Strategically using colors and contrasts directs attention and triggers specific emotions, like calmness with blues or urgency with reds.

Another crucial aspect is a visual hierarchy, which guides visitors along a path that builds interest and leads to conversion. Elements like font size, images, and layout highlight key messages and CTAs, making them the focus of the visitor's journey. Including social proof, such as testimonials or trust badges, adds credibility and reassures visitors about the value they'll get.

Copywriting for Conversions

At the core of every effective landing page is the skill of writing persuasive copy, blending persuasion with clarity to inspire action. The power of this text is based on turning complex offers into compelling stories, focusing on benefits over features and addressing the visitor's desires and challenges directly. Emotional triggers woven into the copy serve as triggers for action, tapping into universal desires like improvement, belonging, and security.

Crafting headlines, a key part of persuasive writing requires accuracy and creativity. They must grab attention and convey value in just a few words. Subheadings and bullet points break down the content into manageable parts, keeping the momentum going and leading the visitor to the call-to-action (CTA) with a mix of information and curiosity. The tone is friendly yet confident, building a connection that makes the visitor feel understood and on the brink of finding a solution that fits their needs perfectly.

A/B Testing for Optimization

A/B testing is vital for optimization, offering a systematic way to understand the audience's preferences through ongoing experiments. This process, far from a one-time fix, is about continuous improvement. Hypotheses are tested, results are analyzed, and adjustments are made with precision. Elements like CTA button color, headline wording, or image choice are tested, each revealing insights into what resonates best with visitors.

This methodical exploration turns intuition into data-driven decisions using tools that segment traffic and track conversions. The result is a landing page that reflects the distilled preferences of visitor engagement, showcasing the marketer's dedication to continuous improvement and quality.

Conversion Rate Optimization (CRO) Techniques

Moving beyond A/B testing, advanced conversion rate optimization (CRO) techniques dive deeply into understanding visitor psychology. CROs use insights from behavioral analytics to shape landing pages that attract and strongly persuade action. Heatmaps and session recordings reveal how visitors interact with the page, highlighting areas of high engagement and spots that get overlooked quickly. This visual data guides changes that improve usability and interaction, like moving CTAs or simplifying forms.

Integrity is valuable in using urgency and scarcity to boost a landing page's persuasive power. These tactics gently push visitors towards action by reminding them of a limited time or the exclusive nature of an offer. Technology-made personalization tailors the landing page experience for each visitor. It shows messages, deals, or testimonials that match their interests and past interactions with the brand.

In creating a highly effective affiliate landing page, every element —from design principles and persuasive writing to testing and advanced optimization techniques—is intentionally chosen. This orchestration of strategies, blending art and science, turns a passive webpage into an engaging stage where visitors actively participate in a story that leads them toward conversion.

10.5 NAVIGATING CHALLENGES AND SETBACKS IN AFFILIATE MARKETING

Uncertainties are common throughout the dynamic affiliate marketing world. Successfully dealing with challenges becomes a key trait of a thriving marketer. This section explores strategies that minimize the impact of these obstacles and turn them into chances for growth and learning.

Dealing with Program Changes

Changes in affiliate programs, such as alterations in commissions or sudden closures, can be unsettling for even experienced marketers. The first step in adapting to these changes is maintaining a diverse range of affiliate programs. This helps reduce risk, ensuring that if one program changes or ends, it doesn't drastically affect overall earnings. Building good communication with affiliate managers can provide insights into upcoming changes, allowing for strategy adjustments beforehand. In cases where a program closes, establishing audience relationships can guide the transition to other products or services, preserving trust and continuity in recommendations.

Overcoming Traffic Fluctuations

Fluctuations in website traffic, crucial for affiliate marketing, can disrupt income and progress. To counter this, focus on SEO resilience ensures a steady flow of organic traffic by creating content around evergreen topics that stay relevant over time. Also, adopting a multi-channel approach to generating traffic through social media, email campaigns, and paid ads creates a safety net against a drop in any single source. Crafting engaging content tailored to each platform and its audience builds community and loyalty, turning temporary visitors into loyal followers.

Addressing Legal and Ethical Issues

With regulations and ethical standards evolving, staying vigilant and adaptable is essential. Keeping up to date with legal changes, especially regarding data protection and privacy, is necessary for continued compliance. Being transparent in communication about affiliate relationships and data use meets regulatory standards and builds audience trust. Ethical marketing is a cornerstone of brand reputation. Regularly auditing marketing practices and affiliate partnerships based on moral principles ensures alignment with legal standards and meets audience expectations.

Recovering from Failures

Setbacks are a natural part of the affiliate marketing journey, whether it's campaigns that don't succeed or goals that aren't met. Dealing with failure starts by looking closely at what went wrong and using introspection to learn and grow. Instead of blaming oneself, find lessons in disappointment and work to understand where strategies didn't work or where the market changed unexpectedly. Armed with this understanding, set smaller, reachable goals and regain confidence through small wins. Having a mindset focused on growth sees obstacles as opportunities to improve rather than as barriers, which builds resilience. Viewing failure as a teacher rather than an enemy brings valuable experience, strength, and a better grasp of the affiliate marketing world's climate.

From diversifying affiliate programs practically to building resilience in generating traffic and adhering to ethical standards, each strategy adds stability and adaptability to the marketer's tool-kit. Furthermore, changing how setbacks are seen from dead ends to steps in the journey adds resilience and a strong desire for growth to the marketer's outlook.

As we conclude this exploration of overcoming challenges in affiliate marketing, we're reminded that setbacks are temporary, but the lessons learned are lasting. These strategies help deal with immediate problems and build lasting resilience, preparing marketers for the difficulties of growth. Each challenge overcome and setback endured strengthens resolve and deepens understanding of the intricate workings of affiliate marketing.

CONCLUSION

As we wrap up this extensive exploration of the vibrant affiliate marketing world, it's important to recognize this dynamic field's incredible potential. Affiliate marketing blends flexibility, scalability, and global reach, offering a unique opportunity for individuals aiming to achieve financial freedom and build significant online income streams. It embodies the promises of the digital era, providing a platform where dedication, strategic thinking, and innovation can synergize to unlock remarkable economic possibilities.

Throughout this book, we've covered the essential steps to excel in affiliate marketing, providing a roadmap for newcomers and experienced marketers. From choosing the right niche and affiliate programs to creating compelling content and mastering SEO and social media strategies, each chapter was designed to equip you with the knowledge and tools needed to thrive in this competitive domain.

Key lessons from our journey emphasize the critical importance of ethical conduct, the continuous pursuit of learning, and the ability to adapt quickly to industry changes. The affiliate marketing narrative is one of growth, requiring patience, persistence, and a commitment to investing time and effort into building a sustainable online business.

As you prepare to embark on your affiliate marketing journey, please take that first confident step forward. Apply the strategies, insights, and lessons shared here. Remember, the affiliate marketing world offers numerous resources, including vibrant online communities, extensive reading materials, webinars, and forums. Dive into these resources, as they are essential for your ongoing education and development in this field.

Let the success stories shared in this book inspire and guide you. They prove that many, like you, started wanting financial independence. Their achievements, fueled by dedication and strategic choices, light the way for your path to success.

Facing challenges and setbacks is inevitable, but with the strategies shared in this book, you can turn each obstacle into a stepping-stone toward growth and achievement. I encourage you to embrace these moments, as they are integral to your journey, making it richer and strengthening your determination.

I welcome you to join the vibrant community formed around this book. Share your experiences, celebrate your progress, and draw inspiration from the collective wisdom of fellow marketers who, like you, navigate the complexities of affiliate marketing. Collaboration and mutual support are key pillars of this journey.

In conclusion, I want to emphasize the importance of integrity and ethical practices in affiliate marketing. Building trust with your audience isn't just a tactic; it's the groundwork for lasting success.

With optimism and knowledge, I urge you to take action. The path to financial freedom, achieving your dreams, and fulfilling your ambitions starts with consistent small steps. You have the tools, insights, and determination to excel in affiliate marketing. Let this not be the end but the beginning of an incredible adventure.

Move forward with courage. The affiliate marketing world is waiting for your unique contribution. Your journey begins now.

MAKE A DIFFERENCE WITH YOUR REVIEW

Dear Reader,

Thank you for joining me on this journey through "Affiliate Marketing for Beginners: Unlock Online Income, Avoid Costly Mistakes & Pitfalls, Create a Solid Foundation for Long-Term Success, and Achieve Financial Independence". I hope you found the book insightful and empowering as you navigate the world of affiliate marketing.

Your feedback is invaluable. By sharing your thoughts and experiences through a review, you can help other readers make informed decisions and embark on their own paths to success. Your review can make a real difference in someone's life.

Please take a moment to leave a review on Amazon. Your words have the power to inspire and guide others, just as this book has inspired and guided you. Let's unlock the power of generosity together and create a community of support and learning.

Thank you for being a part of this journey.

Warm regards, Audrey K. Andado

REFERENCES

References

Advertise Purple. (n.d.). 31+ Essential Affiliate Marketing Tools for 2024. https://www.advertisepurple.com/31-essential-affiliate-marketing-tools/

Affiliate Marketing Case Study (from Zero to $10k Per Month). (n.d.). Contentellect. https://www.contentellect.com/affiliate-marketing-case-study/

Affiliate Marketing Keyword Research: Complete Guide ... Printify Blog. (n.d.). Printify. https://printify.com/blog/affiliate-marketing-keyword-research/

AffiliateWP. (n.d.). A Complete Guide to Setting Affiliate Commission Rates ... https://affiliatewp.com/affiliate-commissions-whats-the-right-approach/

Affiliate marketing. (n.d.). In Wikipedia. https://en.wikipedia.org/wiki/Affiliate_marketing

Ahrefs. (n.d.). 12 SEO Best Practices to Improve Rankings in 2023. https://ahrefs.com/blog/seo-best-practices/

Authority Hacker. (n.d.). How to Build an Email List for Affiliate Marketing (9 Steps). https://www.authorityhacker.com/affiliate-marketing-email-list/

Brady, K. (n.d.). 6 Ways To Effectively Use Social Media For Affiliate Marketing. LinkedIn. https://www.linkedin.com/pulse/6-ways-effectively-use-social-media-affiliate-marketing-kristen-brady-rbhec

Digital Marketing Stream. (n.d.). Boost Sales with AI-driven Marketing. https://digitalmarketingstream.com/marketing-faq/

FTC's Endorsement Guides: What People Are Asking. (n.d.). Federal Trade Commission. https://www.ftc.gov/business-guidance/resources/ftcs-endorsement-guides-what-people-are-asking

Growth Collective. (n.d.). Affiliate Marketing SEO: 13 Practical Tips For Better Results. https://www.growthcollective.com/blog/affiliate-marketing-seo

Hashtag Expert. (n.d.). 7 Success Stories of Affiliate Marketers Who Made Millions. https://www.hashtag.expert/growth/highest-earning-affiliate-marketers

How to Create High Converting Content (9 Tips). (n.d.). Omniscient. https://beomniscient.com/blog/high-converting-content/

How to Create an Effective PPC Strategy in 7 Steps. (n.d.). Semrush. https://www.semrush.com/blog/ppc-strategy/

How to Find a Profitable Niche in Affiliate Marketing. (n.d.). Patel, N. Neil Patel. https://neilpatel.com/blog/find-profitable-niche-affiliate-marketing/

How to Use Video Content to Improve Your Affiliate Marketing Game. (n.d.).

GoAffPro. https://blog.goaffpro.com/how-to-use-video-content-to-improve-your-affiliate-marketing-game/

Influencer Marketing Hub. (n.d.). Top 7 Affiliate Marketing Trends for 2023. https://influencermarketinghub.com/affiliate-marketing-trends/

Influencer Marketing ROI: Calculate ROI And Maximize Your Social Impact. (n.d.). Keyhole. https://keyhole.co/blog/influencer-marketing-roi/

Landingi. (n.d.). Affiliate Marketing Landing Pages: Guide & 5 Examples. https://landingi.com/blog/affiliate-marketing-landing-pages/

Moz. (n.d.). Beginner's Guide to SEO (Search Engine Optimization). https://moz.com/beginners-guide-to-seo

6 Personal Financial Planning Tips Every Entrepreneur Should Know. (n.d.). BrownMiller Wealth Management. https://brownmillerwm.com/6-personal-financial-planning-tips-every-entrepreneur-should-know/

www.ingramcontent.com/pod-product-compliance
Lightning Source LLC
LaVergne TN
LVHW051341050326
832903LV00031B/3664